how to win at poker
belinda levez

For UK order enquiries: please contact Bookpoint Ltd, 130 Milton Park, Abingdon, Oxon OX14 4SB. Telephone: +44 (0)1235 827720. Fax: +44 (0)1235 400454. Lines are open 09.00–18.00, Monday to Saturday, with a 24-hour message answering service. Details about our titles and how to order are available at www.teachyourself.co.uk

For USA order enquiries: please contact McGraw-Hill Customer Services, PO Box 545, Blacklick, OH 43004-0545, USA. Telephone: 1-800-722-4726. Fax: 1-614-755-5645.

For Canada order enquiries: please contact McGraw-Hill Ryerson Ltd, 300 Water St, Whitby, Ontario L1N 9B6, Canada. Telephone: 905 430 5000. Fax: 905 430 5020.

Long-renowned as the authoritative source for self-guided learning – with more than 30 million copies sold worldwide – the *Teach Yourself* series includes over 300 titles in the fields of languages, crafts, hobbies, business, computing and education.

British Library Cataloguing in Publication Data: a catalogue record for this title is available from The British Library.

Library of Congress Catalog Card Number: on file

First published in UK 2001 by Hodder Headline Ltd, 338 Euston Road, London, NW1 3BH.

First published in US 2001 by Contemporary Books, a Division of The McGraw-Hill Companies, 1 Prudential Plaza, 130 East Randolph Street, Chicago, IL 60601, USA.

The 'Teach Yourself' name is a registered trade mark of Hodder & Stoughton Ltd.

Typeset by Transet Limited, Coventry, England.
Printed in Great Britain for Hodder & Stoughton Educational, a division of Hodder Headline Ltd, 338 Euston Road, London NW1 3BH by Cox & Wyman Ltd, Reading, Berkshire.

Papers used in this book are natural, renewable and recyclable products. They are made from wood grown in sustainable forests. The logging and manufacturing processes conform to the environmental regulations of the country of origin.

Impression number   7 6 5 4 3
Year   2009 2008 2007 2006 2005 2004

contents

introduction

Poker is a game which is easy to learn and fun to play. Most people learn to play poker at home with family and friends. The stakes are often low, just piles of matchsticks and your pride. However, playing for money, especially with strangers, is an entirely different experience.

You may have found yourself in the following situation: You are at a party/gathering and get chatting to a stranger. 'Can you play poker?' he asks. The question seems innocent enough, and he appears friendly, so you answer 'Yes' and find yourself invited to play a game. You are introduced to the stranger's friends who warmly welcome you. You feel relaxed and confident, especially after you've won the first couple of pots, but then your luck changes. A few hours later your wallet is lighter and you are wiser. You have learnt that playing poker is easy but winning money at poker is not. You also no longer trust your new friends. You begin to wonder whether or not they were cheating. Some of the hands you were dealt were really good but your opponents always managed to have even better hands. You have just had your first real poker lesson and it cost you a lot of money.

To play poker well takes skill, knowledge and lots of practice. This book aims to teach you how to win at poker. You will be shown the basic principles of the game, and given advice on where to gamble and the associated costs involved. The dangers of playing in private games with strangers are also highlighted and you are shown how to spot cheats. You will be taught how to get better value for money and methods of play that maximize winnings while keeping losses to a minimum. Popular variations of the games are described and strategies given for each game which you should adapt according to the strengths and weaknesses of your opponents.

Lots of illustrated examples are given to make the understanding of the games easier. A glossary is included to define the jargon used in the book and some of the additional jargon that you may encounter.

By the end of this book you should be a more informed player with a better understanding of the game. With plenty of practice you should also become a more skilful player and, hopefully, a winner instead of a loser. Good luck!

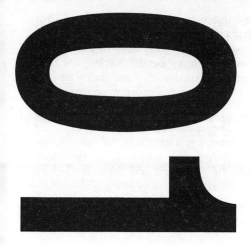

01

what is poker?

In this chapter you will learn:
- why people play poker
- the history of poker
- about famous players

Poker is a name given to a huge number of card games. What they have in common is that they are based on the ranking of five card hands. The basic game is relatively easy to learn. The object of the game is to win the money bet by having the best ranking hand. The games can be played with a minimum of two players but around five to seven players is more practical.

The rules of individual games vary enormously. The number of cards dealt to each player, the methods of betting and the ranking of the hands can all differ. Even games of the same name will often be played in a variety of ways. It is therefore important to ensure that you fully understand the rules before you start playing.

In private games you play against all the other players. In order to win you need to beat all of your opponents. Each player takes turns at being the dealer.

When you play in a casino, you have two options. You can either bet against other players or against the casino. In the former, the casino supplies the dealer, charging a percentage of the pot (the money bet) for this service. A deduction of around ten per cent is common. Alternatively, the casino may make an hourly charge for the use of their facilities. If you decide to play against the casino, the casino is the banker and pays out all bets at fixed odds.

Why play poker?

The main attraction of poker is that it is a game of skill. With many card games you rely totally on the luck of the deal. If you have a good hand you win, if you have a poor hand you lose.

Poker is entirely different. Even if you have the worst possible hand you can still win the game by skilful bluffing – you fool the other players into thinking that you have a good hand.

Poker relies on a good player being able to outwit his opponents. You will need to assess the other players' strategies and make decisions based on your conclusions whilst trying to conceal your own strategy. You will constantly appraise your opponents, looking for signs that tell you whether or not they are bluffing, whilst ensuring that you do not let them guess your likely hand.

A good player can increase his winnings by using strategies which keep other players betting for as long as possible. You will need to decide if your opponents are luring you into betting or whether they are just being cautious. Other strategies rely on forcing players to fold by raising bets. Here you will need to consider why a particular player is raising the stakes. Is it just a scare tactic or does he really hold a good hand? You need to consider how much information you are giving away when you bet. Your decisions will usually be based on experience about what you have learnt about the way your opponents play. All the time you will be assessing your own hand, calculating your chances of winning and deciding your next move.

The origins of poker

The game of poker first appeared in New Orleans sometime during the eighteenth century. It was particularly popular among the French settlers. The origins of the game are not documented but it probably evolved from a combination of other card or dice games.

After the arrival of playing cards in Europe in the fourteenth century, new games were continually being invented and adapted. Rules were rarely written down. There are several European card games with similarities to poker. These include the French game of poque, the German game of pochen, the English game of brag and the Italian game of primero. None of these games is a direct descendent of poker but they have most likely had an influence on it. The term 'flush' for example, comes from primero, which dates from the sixteenth century. In primero, four cards of the same suit was called a flux leading to the term flush, which is used in poker to denote a hand of the same suit. The name for poker was probably derived from the French game poque.

The game that has the greatest similarity to poker is the Persian game of As Nas, which dates from the sixteenth century. It was played with a deck of 25 cards with five suits. Each player would initially be dealt two cards. A round of betting would follow. A further two cards were dealt followed by a round of betting. A fifth card would be dealt, followed by another round of betting. Hands were ranked in a similar way to poker. The highest-ranking hand was five of the same suit (equivalent to a flush in poker) followed by five of a kind. A full house of three of a kind with a pair also features in the ranking. As well as betting the game also allowed players to bluff.

It is also possible that poker was adapted from dice games. Poker is based on the ranking of hands. Dice games with the same principle, the ranking of throws, have been played for at least 2000 years. A Roman dice game called tali is based on the ranking of throws where three of a kind beats a pair, much like poker.

The first written account of poker comes from the diary of Joseph Crowell, an English actor, who was touring America in 1829. He described it as a game where players each received five cards and made bets. The highest combination of cards won.

In 1834, Jonathan H. Green gave an account of what he called 'the cheating game' in his book, *An Exposure of the Arts and Miseries of Gambling*. He saw it being played while travelling on a steamboat on the Mississippi river, which was heading for New Orleans. A deck of 20 cards was used with each player receiving a hand of five. The player with the highest-ranking hand would win. The hands were ranked as pairs, three of a kind and four of kind. This early form of poker featured no draws. The players simply received five cards face down and would bet on the cards received.

The 20-card deck was replaced by a 32-card deck and by 1833 a 52-card deck had been introduced. Brief mentions of poker were made in *Hoyles' Games* in 1850 where it was described as a game for ten players where each player received five cards face down.

The spread of poker

New Orleans had numerous gambling establishments where poker was played including the Crescent City House, a luxury casino, which was opened by John Davis in 1827. As America was settled poker spread and was played on boats that travelled along the Mississippi and Ohio rivers. Professional gamblers known as sharps made their living by playing cards with riverboat passengers and relieving them of their money. Cheating was rife.

Poker spread to the west by settlers who travelled on wagon trains. When gold was discovered in California in 1848, gambling flourished in the prospecting camps. San Francisco, which became a huge tented city, had over 1000 gambling houses where gold was the currency. Initially games like roulette were most popular but gradually card games such as poker caught on.

The game spread rapidly during the Civil War (1861–5). Soldiers would play poker to pass time. Lack of money resulted in them fashioning gaming chips out of flattened bullets and pieces of bone. The soldiers would usually discard their playing cards before battle as they were considered to be 'instruments of the devil' and the soldiers did not want to die carrying them. It was during the Civil War that stud poker first emerged.

Lots of variations of the game started to appear which could be divided broadly into two types, draw poker and stud poker. In draw poker all the cards are dealt face down and seen only by the player of the hand. Players are then allowed to exchange cards to improve their hand. In stud poker some of the cards are dealt face up on the table and players make a hand by combining their cards and those on the table. New rankings of hands and betting methods were also incorporated. In the 1867 edition of *Hoyles' Games*, a straight and a straight flush and an ante had been incorporated into the game. By 1875, jackpot poker and the use of a joker as a wild card had been mentioned.

Poker players made a living travelling from town to town. Virtually every saloon of the Old West had a poker table where a buckhorn knife would be passed around the table to denote the dealer. This led to the phrase 'passing the buck'. Later a silver dollar was used which gave rise to the slang term of 'a buck for a dollar'. Disputes over the game were often settled with a gun. A famous poker player from this time was Doc Holliday (1851–87) who on several occasions got into a gunfight over poker.

Poker arrived in England in 1872. It was introduced by Robert C. Schenk, the American Ambassador to England. He had been invited to a party at a country house in Somerset where he had taught his fellow guests how to play poker. The hostess persuaded him to write down the rules, which were then published. The game was popular among the aristocracy and became know as Schenk poker. Queen Victoria is known to have played the game as a diversion after the death of her husband, Prince Albert.

In 1911, legislation was passed in the United States that prohibited stud poker as it was concluded that it was a game of luck. However, a ruling was passed that draw poker was a game of skill and therefore not illegal. As this led to the decline of stud poker, new draw games were invented.

Prohibition in the 1920s was responsible for poker becoming a home-based game. With the closure of drinking and gaming establishments, private games were organized and became part of American culture. The traditional venue became the kitchen table where family and friends would gather to play. The playing of private games resulted in lots of variations, with each household inventing their own rules. New rankings of hands, incorporation of one or more wild cards and different ways of organizing the betting were introduced.

When gambling was legalized in Nevada in the 1930s, draw poker was introduced to Las Vegas casinos. In 1970, Benny Binion, owner of the Horseshoe Casino in Las Vegas, decided to hold a poker tournament so that the best players in the world could compete against each other. The tournament, called the World Series of Poker, has become an annual event with players from around the globe competing. The game chosen for the championship was Texas hold 'em, resulting in it becoming one of the most widely played games.

In the mid-1980s Caribbean stud poker was invented on the Caribbean island of Aruba. It began to be played on cruise ships and gradually spread to casinos around the world. It differs from other poker games as it is played against the casino which acts as banker. Instead of playing for a pot the winning hands are paid out at fixed odds. There is also no bluffing involved.

Poker has also been played on gaming machines since the 1800s. In 1891 Sittman and Pitt of Brooklyn began manufacturing poker card machines. They proved extremely popular and were installed in virtually all of Brooklyn's licensed liquor establishments, which at that time numbered over 3000. By 1901 the machines had been redesigned so that draw poker could be played.

In the mid-1970s video poker was invented. By 1976, the first black and white video poker machines appeared. They were superseded eight months later with a colour version. Nowadays video poker is one of the most popular casino games.

With the innovation of the internet, on-line poker was invented. Computer technology allows players from all over the world to compete against each other from the comfort of their own homes. Gaming sites offer traditional poker, video poker and Caribbean stud poker.

Poker today

Poker is played around the world in private homes, casinos, card clubs and on the internet. It is estimated that poker is more popular than golf, fishing, football or basketball. The World Series of Poker attracts over 4000 players from around the world. A television audience of over 40 million watches the tournament. In Great Britain and Europe there has been a rise in the popularity of poker mostly due to tournaments being televised.

Casinos around the world offer a wide choice of poker games including five card stud, seven card stud, Texas hold 'em and omaha. In addition, many more casinos have Caribbean stud poker, which is played as a banker game against the casino. Poker is also played widely on video poker machines. Around ten per cent of visitors to Las Vegas casinos bet on video poker machines. This is more than play roulette, craps or keno. Poker is also played with dice as a pub game, which is particularly popular in continental Europe.

Famous poker players

In 1979, a poker hall of fame was founded to honour top poker players. Each year one player is added. Those winning the World Series gain entry. Other members have been given honorary membership. Players in the Poker Hall of Fame include:

- Benny Binion (1904–89) was a former cowboy, gambler and owner of the Horseshoe Casino, the venue for the World Series. He was an all-round player, skilled at many forms of poker.
- Doyle 'Texas Dolly' Brunson gave up a career as a salesman to become a professional poker player in the 1950s when he realized that he could earn ten times his salary in a fraction of the time at the tables. He practised the game for up to 20 hours a day and started out playing in backroom card games. He won $600,000 as winner of the World Series in 1976 and 1977.
- 'Nick the Greek' Dandolos (1893–1966) became famous for his huge bets. His gambling career started after he won $500,000 in six months betting on horse racing. He then took up card and dice games where he lost his fortune. Undaunted he decided to study card games and reportedly won over $6 million at stud poker throughout his career.
- 'Wild Bill' Hickok was a poker player with a short but eventful life. He was a scout during the Civil War, a marshal in Kansas and toured in Buffalo Bill's Wild West Show as a sharpshooter. He was shot in the back during a poker game by Crooked Nose McCall on 2 August 1876. The hand that he was holding at the time, a pair of aces over eights, has gone down in poker legend as the dead man's hand.
- Johnny Moss – three times winner of the World Series in 1970, 1971 and 1974 – once played a five-month long game with Nick the Greek, taking breaks only for sleep. Moss won an estimated $2 million.

02

playing tips

In this chapter you will learn:
- how to stay solvent
- costs of playing
- body language

Taking a sensible approach to gambling

Before you begin gambling, you should work out a financial budget. Calculate all your household and living costs including savings. Realistically work out how much money you can comfortably afford to lose – yes *lose*. Gambling is risky, not everyone wins, and there are plenty of losers. You can easily lose all of your capital. Be aware that there are much easier, more profitable and safer ways of making money.

Once you have decided your budget, make sure you never go over this limit. If your personal circumstances change, be sure to re-calculate. If you spend only disposable income on gambling, you won't encounter many problems. However, if you start betting with your rent money and lose it, you may be tempted to try to recoup your losses by betting more heavily. This is the route to financial ruin.

When you play, take only your stake money and enough for your expenses (fare home, drinks, meals etc.). Leave all cheque books and cash cards at home. If you can't get hold of more money, you can't spend it. Don't be tempted to borrow money from friends, and be sure to decline all offers of credit. If you run out of money, either go home or just spectate.

If you don't want to carry large amounts of cash, open a separate account for your gambling money and take with you only the cheque book and cards relating to that account when you gamble.

Exchanging money for chips

In most games, particularly in casinos, you exchange your money for chips. You don't play with 'real money', just a pile of plastic discs. Psychologically the value of your money diminishes. When you see a bank note, you associate it with its true value – you appreciate how long it would take you to earn that amount of money and what you can buy with it. As soon as you exchange it for chips, those associations disappear. It is no accident that chips resemble coins – coins are considered almost worthless. It's easy to pick up a pile of chips and put them on a bet. If you had to count out bank notes, you would certainly be more cautious.

When you decide to play, don't immediately change all of your money into chips. Instead, change it in small amounts. If you have to keep going to your wallet, you will have a better appreciation of how much you are losing as you will be watching real money diminish rather than chips.

If you win, it's all too easy to give your winnings back by continuing to play. If you are playing in a casino, as soon as is convenient, go to the cash point and change your cash chips back into money. Once you see the true value, you will be more reluctant to carry on betting.

People like to have piles of chips in front of them – it makes them look like a high roller. Walk around a casino and see the proud smiles when someone has a big pile of chips. However, you should only have in front of you the amount of chips that you need to play.

What does it cost to play?

Once you have calculated your budget you need to find a game that is compatible with your level of stakes. If the stakes are too high you will find yourself quickly running out of money.

The minimum amount of capital you need varies depending on the game. As a rough guide, the capital needed for a game of draw poker is around 40 times the minimum stake. With seven card stud approximately 50 times the minimum stake should be sufficient. Games like hold 'em and omaha need around 100 times the minimum stake. By dividing the amount that you have budgeted for by the minimum capital required, you can find the minimum stakes that you can play for.

The minimum stakes on many poker games are low. You should be able to find somewhere to play to suit your budget. You don't have to be a high roller to go to a casino. Most casinos have plenty of low stake tables. If you prefer to play in private games, you should be able to find one that suits your level of stakes.

Do not aim too high when you are still learning. Even if your budget allows you to play in the more expensive games, stick initially to the cheaper games and gradually work your way up. Remember, the higher the stakes the better the players.

Additional costs

It's all too easy to go over your budget by forgetting to include all the costs. Casino gambling has additional hidden costs which include things like:

- house advantage
- commission

- admission charges
- membership fees
- travelling costs
- refreshments
- your time

Commission

Casinos charge gamblers for the use of their facilities. With poker, a percentage of the pot is taken by the house. This is a small price to pay when you consider that you are guaranteed a fairly run game. Around ten per cent is the usual deduction. For bigger games players are often charged an hourly rate for their seat.

House advantage

In games where the casino acts as a banker, a hidden charge is made for the privilege of betting. Many people don't even realize that there is a charge for gambling. On many games like Caribbean stud poker you are not paid the true odds. The casino reduces the odds paid to allow it to make a profit.

Finding your game

It is a good idea to try playing a variety of games at home. Decide which game you like the best and, once you have selected your favourite, concentrate solely on that game. Try to watch as many games as possible – you can learn a great deal by watching experienced players. If someone is winning, try to determine why. Are they just lucky or are they using a particular strategy? Are their stakes varied or constant? What do they do when they lose – do they increase or reduce their stakes or stop playing?

Check the rules before you start playing

Learn how to play a game before you bet on it. This may seem common sense, but a lot of people start playing poker with no understanding of the rules. Often they are introduced to poker by friends or relations and they simply bet in the same manner as their friends. They end up learning by their mistakes which can be costly.

Remember, the rules of poker vary enormously. Ensure you fully understand all the rules before you play. Casinos will have written copies of their rules available. Take them home and study them at your leisure. If you don't understand them, ask for an explanation. Whatever game you select, find out as much information about it as possible.

You need to be particularly careful with private games as rules may differ enormously. Just knowing the name of a game is not sufficient as players often introduce variations.

Have a full discussion about the rules before you start playing. It is often a good idea to write down the rules that you have been told to avoid later disputes about what was actually said before play commenced.

Pay particular attention to the ranking of hands as you may find that hands other than the standard rankings are permitted. Ensure that you fully understand the method of betting and whether or not checking is allowed (see page 18). Agree both minimum and maximum bets. If wild cards are used, check if additional hands like five of a kind count in the ranking.

The lollapalooza

John Lillard's *Poker Stories* (1896) recounts the tale of a cheat playing a game of poker in a Montana saloon. He deals himself a hand of four aces and ends up betting against an old prospector. The prospector bets all of his money against the cheat. When the hands are revealed the prospector has only an assortment of clubs and diamonds which is not a ranking poker hand. The cheat starts counting his winnings, only to be stopped by the old man. He explains that a lollapalooza beats any other poker hand and that three clubs and two diamonds is in fact a lollapalooza. The other players agree with him so the cheat concedes the win. Later in the game, the cheat deals himself a lollapalooza. He bets heavily on his hand. At the showdown he reveals his hand expecting to take the pot. He is then informed that he should ask the rules before playing as a lollapalooza can only be played once a night.

Get plenty of practice

You need to be able to recognize immediately the value of your hand and where it comes in the ranking. Deal out hands of five cards, identify the poker hands and put them in the correct ranking order. You will soon appreciate how infrequently a good hand is dealt. Once you have mastered the ranking you can then start to judge whether or not a hand is worth playing.

Get plenty of practice. Take a pack of cards and deal out dummy hands as if you're playing the game with several players. Look at your own hand. Decide whether or not it is worth playing. Then assess your hand against the others. Did you make a good decision? Would any of the other hands have beaten yours? Are you throwing away hands that could easily win? By continuing to do this you will learn the sort of hands that are worthwhile playing and those that are not.

Play alone or with friends until you are familiar with all situations. Practise placing bets as you play. Some games are played so quickly that it can be difficult for a novice to follow them. With practice you will become faster.

As mentioned earlier, it is important to play at the right level. Don't aim too high when you are still learning. Stick to the cheaper games and gradually work your way up. Remember, the higher the stakes the better the players.

Other considerations

Poker relies on the other players not knowing your hand. Although the other players cannot see your hand, the way that you react to its contents can give them a lot of information.

Body language

Suppose you have a really good hand. It is quite likely that as you look at the cards you will smile, raise your eyebrows or constantly look at your cards. You know that this time you are certain of a winning hand. When you're excited your voice also changes. The other players will notice and probably fold, meaning that your good hand will win you very little money.

If, alternatively, you have a poor hand, you are more likely to frown. You may decide to try bluffing, but if you appear nervous, fidgety or start playing with your chips, the other players are less likely to believe you. You may even give one of the classic signs of lying, such as touching your nose. When you are nervous you are also more likely to stutter.

People who have complete control over their mannerisms make better poker players. If you can look at your cards and show no facial expressions whatsoever you make it impossible for other players to glean any information about your hand. When you look at your hand, memorize its contents. Pay attention to your mannerisms – don't fiddle with your chips or your jewellery. Stay calm, even if you have a royal flush. If you play and bet confidently you are more likely to intimidate the other players.

One of the most difficult reactions to control is blushing, but you can use this to your advantage. Ask other players direct questions about their hands. If you correctly guess their hand they may blush. However, be prepared for other players to ask you questions. A confident reply may confuse them.

Keep records

Keep records of your gambling. A small notebook is sufficient to keep records of how much you win and lose. Most people tend to remember the big wins and forget the losses. After each game write down the reasons why you won or lost. Analyse the results and learn from your mistakes.

If you lost, try to determine why. Were you staying in when you should have folded? Were you folding with hands that could have won? Were you failing to force other players into folding? Was your body language giving away information?

When you win also try to determine the reasons why. Was it because your strategy was good? Were you just dealt lots of good hands? Did other players make stupid mistakes? Were you picking up on any signs given by the other players?

Periodically analyse your records. They will tell you if you're sticking to your budget and if your betting strategy is effective. Proper records will make you aware of any weaknesses. You can then alter your strategy to compensate.

Player profiles

If you play regularly with the same people, try to build up a profile of each one.

- What sort of hands do they bet heavily on?
- What forces them to fold?
- How often do they bluff?
- Does their body language give any clues?
- How do they bet with a good hand?

Try to work out each player's strategy.

Appreciate your chances of winning

Many people expect to win but don't realistically assess their chances of winning. With all bets there is the chance that you will lose, and it is important to understand how to calculate your chances of winning. You may decide that a bet is simply not worthwhile.

Learn how to calculate the odds for the game that you are playing. Fully appreciate your chances of improving hands. Before you place a bet, make sure you understand your chances of winning. If you are playing in a casino do not forget to take into account the rake (the charge made by the casino for the use of its facilities).

With banking games find both the true odds (your chances of winning) and the odds paid by the casino. Is there a huge difference? You may decide that it is not worth your while having a bet.

Vary your play

Players use different styles of play. Some play aggressively, continually raising in an attempt to force everyone to fold. Other players are very cautious, throwing away anything that is not a good hand. You will know when they suddenly make a huge bet that they have a good hand.

Try not to stick to one style of playing. The most successful poker players are those who are totally unpredictable. If in some hands you play cautiously and in others aggressively you will confuse the opposition. You should aim to vary your betting, the number of cards you take (if playing a draw game), how often you bluff and the signals that you give.

Know when to stop gambling

It can take an enormous amount of discipline to stop betting, particularly if you are on a winning streak. It is possible to get carried away by the excitement of the game. You may have intended to spend only an hour gambling but you're on a winning streak, so you continue. Because you are betting with your winnings rather than the initial stake money, you decide to place larger bets. Your next bet loses, what do you do? For a lot of people the tendency is to bet more heavily to recoup that loss. This will usually continue until you run out of funds.

If you have lost your stake money, decline all offers of credit. Even if the other players agree to accept an IOU, you should withdraw from the game. Stories abound of people who have run out of money and who have ended up throwing their car keys or the promise of some other asset into the pot. If the stakes are getting too high or you are losing too much, stop playing. By having a sensible approach to gambling you can ensure that you do not lose more than you can afford.

The majority of gamblers are able to keep to their budgets. However, gambling can be addictive for some people so beware. If you start losing more than you can afford, seek help. Details of organizations that can help are given at the end of the book.

Try to decide in advance at what stage you are going to stop betting. Set yourself an amount to win or lose or impose a time limit. Stop playing when you have reached your limit. As soon as a winning streak stops either bet small stakes or go home. This approach will minimize your losses. Other players may complain if you suddenly stop playing, but remember you are not betting for their benefit. Do not feel obliged to give them the opportunity to win their money back.

You should always stop playing if you are tired. You need to ensure that you are concentrating on the game. When you are tired, you take longer to make decisions and are more likely to make mistakes.

It is also wise to avoid alcohol. It tends to slow down your reactions and your ability to think. It also lowers your inhibitions, and makes you less likely to care about losses. You should certainly never play if you are drunk.

03

the basic game

In this chapter you will learn:
- the basics of poker
- the ranking of hands
- additional markings

One deck of 52 cards with the jokers removed is used. Before any cards are dealt, players make an initial bet called an ante-bet. This helps to increase the pot. It also makes the game more competitive as players are more likely to try to win the pot if they have contributed to it. All the bets are placed in the centre of the table. In casinos, players exchange their stake money for chips. With private games bets are often made with cash but some schools may use chips to facilitate betting.

Each player receives five cards dealt face down. A round of blind betting may take place (players make a bet without looking at their cards). This further increases the pot. Players look at their cards. A round of betting commences starting with the player to the left of the dealer (in forms of poker where some cards are placed face up, the player with the highest or lowest card may bet first).

Each player has the option of betting or folding (withdrawing from the game). A player holding a poor hand may decide to fold. If you fold, your cards are returned to the dealer without being revealed to the other players. You lose any bets made.

Some games allow players to 'check'. This usually happens on the first round of betting after the cards have been dealt. Players do not have to participate in the first round of betting, instead they announce 'check'. If they wish to continue in the game they must bet on their next turn. If all the players decide to check, new hands are dealt to everyone. Some players use checking as a strategy for bluffing. They have a good hand but do not want to make it obvious on the first round of betting. When it is their turn to make a bet, they raise the stakes. This strategy is called 'sandbagging'. However, if you have a fairly decent hand, it can be a risky strategy to check. If all the other players check you will lose out on a pot that you may have won.

The first bet determines how much each player has to bet in order to stay in the game. Players may also raise the bet up to the agreed maximum. Betting continues until either only one player remains or there is a showdown and players reveal their hands. If only one player remains (all the others have folded), he will win the pot. He does not reveal his cards to the other players. If there is a showdown, the player with the highest ranking poker hand wins the pot. In the event of a tie the pot is shared. In a showdown (Figure 3.1), player D would win as he has the highest ranking hand.

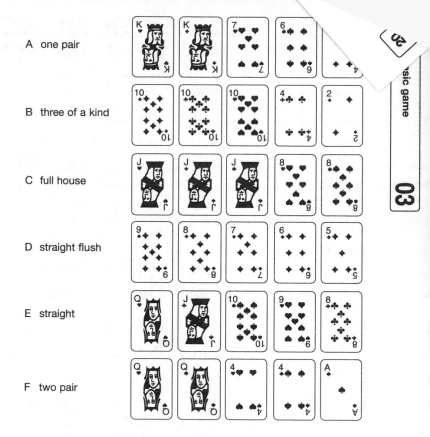

A one pair

B three of a kind

C full house

D straight flush

E straight

F two pair

figure 3.1 example hands

The standard ranking of hands

The aim of poker is to win the pot by having the highest ranking hand. A poker hand is made up from five cards. The more difficult a hand is to achieve, the higher its position in the ranking. Figure 3.2 shows how the hands are ranked.

Each type of hand is also ranked according to the values of the cards. The highest value cards are aces and the lowest are twos. The cards are ranked in the following descending order: A, K, Q, J, 10, 9, 8, 7, 6,5 , 4, 3, 2. The suits do not affect the ranking, so if two players both have a royal flush, one with hearts and one

royal flush

straight flush

four of a kind

full house

flush

straight

three of a kind

two pair

one pair

no pair, highest card

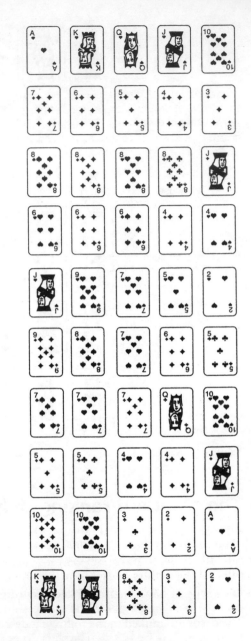

figure 3.2 poker hands ranked from highest to lowest

with spades, the hands will tie. However, if you play in a private game, you may find that the players introduce their own rules which rank the suits differently. Always check the rankings before you play.

The highest ranking hand is a royal flush – A, K, Q, J, 10 in the same suit. There are only four ways that this hand can be made, with hearts, diamonds, spades or clubs. If you are dealt this hand, you know that you have the highest ranking hand and can not be beaten by any other player.

A straight flush is a run of five cards of the same suit in consecutive numerical order. If two players both have a straight flush, the player with the highest card wins so K, Q, J, 10, 9 beats Q, J, 10, 9, 8.

Four of a kind is four cards of the same numerical value with any other card. Four aces is the highest ranking four of a kind and will beat four kings.

A full house is three of a kind (three cards of the same value) and a pair (two cards of the same value). Where two players have a full house, the hand with the highest value for the three of a kind wins. So 10, 10, 10, 2, 2 would beat 8, 8, 8, A, A.

A flush is a run of five cards of the same suit in any numerical order. Where two players have a flush, the one with the highest card wins. So J, 8, 6, 5, 3 would beat 9, 8, 6, 5, 4.

A straight is five cards of any suit in consecutive numerical order. A, K, Q, J, 10 is the highest straight followed by K, Q, J, 10, 9. Where two players both have a straight, the hand with the highest card wins.

Three of a kind is three cards of the same numerical value with two cards of different values. Three sixes would beat three fours.

Two pair is two sets of pairs (two cards with the same value) with any other card. Where two players both have two pair, the value of the highest pair decides the winner. A, A, 3, 3, 2 would beat 10, 10, 8, 8, A. If both players have the same two pair, the value of the fifth card decides the winner. K, K, Q, Q, 8 would beat K, K, Q, Q, 4. If all cards have the same value there is a tie.

One pair is two cards of the same value with three other cards of different values. A pair of queens would beat a pair of jacks. If two players have the same pair, the hand with the highest value other cards wins. A, A, 10, 7, 5 would beat A, A, 9, 7, 5. If all of the cards are of the same value then there is a tie.

Where none of the above hands is held, the winner is the player with the highest card. In a showdown a hand containing an ace would beat one with a king and so on.

Low poker

The ranking described so far is for high poker. It is also possible to play low poker, where the lowest ranking hand wins – known as the 'wheel' or the 'bicycle'. Other games exist where players compete for both the highest hand and the lowest hand. They usually nominate what hand they are playing for. Here the pot will be split, half for the highest hand and half for the lowest hand.

Figure 3.3 shows how the low hands are ranked. Before playing these games, you should check what the lowest rankings are as they may vary.

Additional rankings

It is always important to check the ranking of the hands before you play as some games include additional hands. In private games you may come across one or more of the hands described below. (See Figure 3.4 for examples.)

Skeet/pelter

These hands come between a flush and a straight in the ranking. It is commonly 9, 5, 2 and two other cards below 9 of any combination of suits. However, some games specify that the two other cards must include one card between 9 and 5 and the other card between 5 and 2. If the cards are all the same suit, you have a skeet flush which ranks higher than a straight flush.

Dutch/skip straight or kilter

This is an alternately numbered straight. For example, 10, 8, 6, 4, 2 or K, J, 9, 7, 5. It ranks lower than a straight but higher than three of a kind.

the 'wheel'
or 'bicycle'

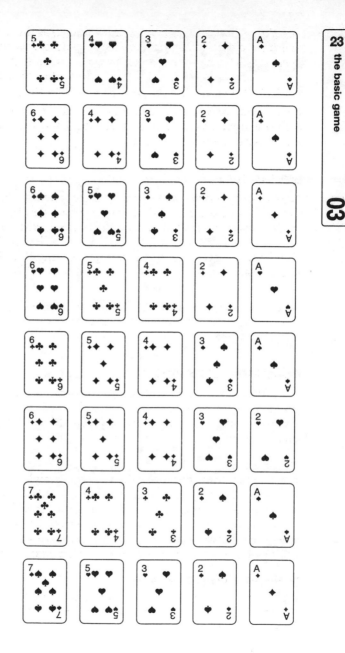

figure 3.3 the ranking of hands in low poker

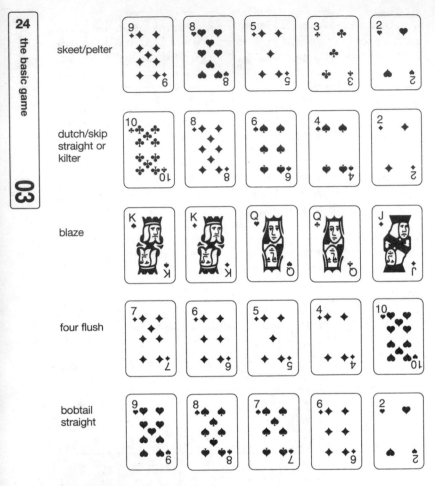

skeet/pelter

dutch/skip
straight or
kilter

blaze

four flush

bobtail
straight

figure 3.4 additional rankings

Blaze

This is a combination of any five court cards that do not contain
three of a kind. For example, K, K, Q, Q, J or Q, Q, J, J, K. It
ranks higher than two pair but lower than three of a kind.
Where this hand is allowed it would, for example, beat A, A, 9,
9, 7.

Four flush

This hand consists of four cards of the same suit, for example,
7, 6, 5, 4 of diamonds and 10 of clubs. It ranks higher than a
pair and lower than two pair.

Bobtail straight

This hand consists of four consecutive cards of any suit and ranks below a four flush. For example, 9 of hearts, 8 of spades, 7 of spades, 6 of diamonds and 2 of hearts.

Cats and dogs

The following hands rank between a flush and a straight. If they are permitted, always check exactly where they come in the ranking as their position may vary. None of the hands must contain a pair. (See Figure 3.5 for examples.)

Big cat/tiger

This hand consists of a king and an 8 with three other cards with a value between a king and an 8.

Little cat/tiger

This hand should have an 8 and a 3 with the three other cards having a value between an 8 and a 3.

Big dog

This hand needs an ace and a 9 with the three other cards having a value between an ace and a 9.

Little dog

This hand consists of a 7 and a 2 with the three other cards having a value between 7 and 2.

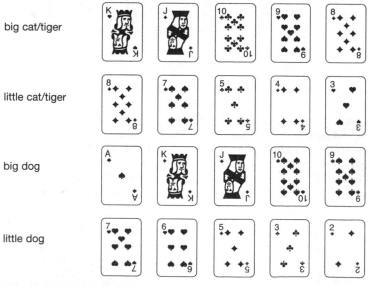

figure 3.5 additional rankings – cats and dogs

Five of a kind

In private games, it is common to allow the use of 'wild' cards. A wild card is a nominated card which can be used in the place of any other card. For example, the twos may be declared 'wild'. If you needed an ace to make up a hand, you could use a 2 instead of an ace. Alternatively, one or more jokers may be added to the pack and declared wild. If, for example, you needed a queen to make up a hand, you could use the joker in its place. By allowing cards to be wild, higher ranking hands are easier to achieve.

When wild cards are allowed, an additional hand of five of a kind is also possible (see Figure 3.6). Five of a kind ranks higher than a royal flush. If you are playing with wild cards always check that five of a kind is permitted as some games may specify that the wild card can only be used in place of another card, which excludes this possibility.

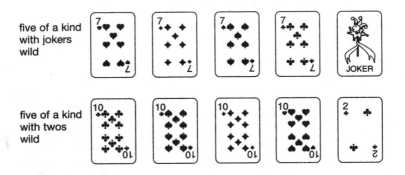

five of a kind with jokers wild

five of a kind with twos wild

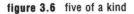

figure 3.6 five of a kind

The basic game of poker is easy to learn. This is poker in its simplest form, but it is hardly ever played in this manner. Lots of variations have been introduced to make the games more exciting and challenging. There is a huge number of different games where both the rules and the methods of betting vary. Games of the same name may be played in a huge variety of ways in different locations. Gamblers who play regularly together may also add their own rules to create more excitement.

The number of cards dealt to each player varies with different games. Some games allow the players to improve their hands by taking extra cards, these are the draw games. Other forms exist where some cards are placed face up on the table. Either some of the players' cards are revealed or players use community cards combined with their own cards to make up the best hand. These are the stud games.

04 understanding the odds

In order to play poker well a sound understanding of the odds of being dealt particular hands is essential. With games like draw poker you need to know the chances of improving your hand. As private games incorporate so many variations, it is important to understand how changes in the rules affect the odds.

In standard games of poker 52 cards are used to make five card hands. There are $\underline{52 \times 51 \times 50 \times 49 \times 48}$ = 2,598,960 different possible hands. $1 \times 2 \times 3 \times 4 \times 5$

The likelihood of being dealt a particular hand in poker

Hand	Number of ways hand can be made	Odds against being dealt cards in your first hand
Royal flush	4	649,739/1
Straight flush	36	72,192/1
Four of a kind	624	4,164/1
Full house	3,744	693/1
Flush	5,108	508/1
Straight	10,200	254/1
Three of a kind	54,912	46/1
Two pair	123,552	20/1
One pair	1,098,240	15/1
Highest card	1,302,540	1/1

To appreciate just how rare the higher ranking hands are, consider how long it takes to play 649,740 hands. If you play, for example, an average of one hand every five minutes, you would need to continue playing constantly for approximately six years and two months. By playing for a few hours each week the chances of being dealt a royal flush in your first hand are something short of a miracle.

Take a pack of cards and deal them out into five card poker hands. By continually repeating this you will begin to appreciate just how rare it is to be dealt one of the higher ranking hands. You will start to get some idea about which hands are worth playing. Pairs are very common. Pairs appear very low down in the ranking but a high pair can often be sufficient to win a game.

If poker is played with only five cards dealt and no further cards exchanged for others from the pack, players are mostly competing with low ranking hands. This is one of the main reasons why so many variations exist. By increasing the number of cards dealt to each player or allowing players to exchange some of the cards for new ones from the pack, the chances of having a higher ranking hand are increased. The varied games add more interest and excitement.

How the odds change with different games

Poker can be played in a wide variety of ways. A different number of cards may be dealt and the number of cards players can exchange may vary. To have a good knowledge of the odds for your particular game you need to take these factors into consideration in your calculations. Before agreeing to any change in the rules ensure that you fully appreciate how the change will affect the odds.

Draw games

When you are playing draw poker, you have the opportunity to improve your hand by exchanging your cards for others from the deck. Before betting and exchanging cards, you will want to know your chances of improving your hand so that you can decide if it is worthwhile staying in the game.

You can calculate your chances of improving your hand by comparing the number of ways in which your desired cards can be dealt to the total number of possible ways in which the remaining cards can be dealt.

The chances of improving a hand when three of a kind is held

Suppose your hand is K, K, K, 6, 3. By exchanging your last two cards, you have the opportunity to make either a full house or four of a kind. For the full house you need a pair and for four of a kind another king is required.

There are four cards of the same value in each suit. Each value can be arranged in six different ways (see Figure 4.1).

figure 4.1 ways in which a pair of fours can be made

There are thirteen different values in total, from ace to 2. As you already hold the kings you are left with a possible twelve other values from which to make a pair. A pair can be made in 72 ways ($6 \times 12 = 72$). You are discarding two cards which reduces the number of ways a pair can be made by five. You therefore have $72 - 5 = 67$ ways in which you can make a full house.

You currently hold five cards, leaving 47 other possible cards ($52 - 5 = 47$). Even though some of the other cards have been dealt to other players, you do not know what cards they hold, so you need to take all possibilities into account when making your calculations. With 47 cards there are 1081 ways in which two cards can be dealt $\left(\dfrac{47 \times 46}{1 \times 2} = 1081 \right)$.

Your chances of improving your hand to make a full house are therefore $(1081 - 67) / 67$ or 1009/67 or odds of approximately 15/1.

To improve the hand to four of a kind you need the last king. By exchanging one card, you are giving yourself odds of 46/1. By exchanging two cards, your odds of having the king are 46/2 or 23/1.

The chances of making four of a kind by drawing three cards to a pair

Suppose your hand is A, A, 7, 9, 4. With three cards there are a possible 16,215 hands $\dfrac{47 \times 46 \times 45}{1 \times 2 \times 3} = 16{,}215.$

The hand you want to be dealt is A, A, X, where 'X' is any other card. A, A, X can be made in 45 ways, where 'X' is any of the other 45 cards.

Your chances of being dealt this hand are (16215 – 45) / 45 or 359/1. You can see that the chances of making this hand are remote.

The chances of making a full house by drawing one card to two pair

If Q, Q, J, J, 10 is held, you need either a queen or a jack for a full house. You exchange one card. There are 47 possible cards that could be dealt to you. Four of them would give you the desired hand (the other two jacks or the other two queens) – 43 of them would not. The odds are 43/4 = 10.75/1.

The chances of making a flush when one card is needed

Suppose your hand is K, 9, 4, 2 of hearts and 10 of diamonds. Your chances of getting another heart to make the flush are as follows: there are nine hearts left which would give you the desired hand and 38 other cards. Your chances of having a heart are 38/9 = 4.33/1.

There is a general rule that says if you get nothing in your first deal you should fold. If you study the table of odds for improving hands you can see the reasoning behind this rule. You may dream of turning a pair into four of a kind but in reality it is very difficult to achieve.

Stud games

In games like seven card stud and hold 'em, a five card poker hand is made from seven cards. With seven cards you are able to make up 21 different five card poker hands. This hugely improves each player's chances of achieving a higher ranking hand. By looking at the cards that each player is showing, or the community cards, you can deduce the possible hand that they may hold and calculate the chances of them having that particular hand.

With omaha, nine cards are used to make a five card poker hand. Therefore 84 different five card poker hands can be made by each player which makes it even easier to achieve a high ranking poker hand.

A pair of aces may have been enough to win a game of five card stud, but in omaha, a pair of aces is highly likely to be beaten.

You are also able to adjust any calculations about players' hands by taking into account the cards that you hold and those which the other players have on display. Consider a game of seven card stud, where four cards of each player's hand are displayed.

A player may have two queens and two jacks displayed. In order to make a full house, he needs either another jack or another queen in his hand. If you have a queen in your hand and another player has a jack displayed, then a full house with queens and jacks can only be made from two other cards, the remaining jack or queen.

If there are five players, 20 cards are displayed, and you also have three cards in your hand. That leaves 29 other cards. Two cards would give a full house. This means the player has odds of 13.5/1 against having a full house (29 − 2) / 2 = 13.5/1.

If no jacks or queens were displayed by other players, or in your hand, the odds against him having a full house with jacks and queens would be (29 − 4)/4 = 6.25/1. You can see that taking into account the cards held by you or displayed by other players can make a big difference to the odds.

The effect of using wild cards

In some games, wild cards may be permitted. A wild card is a card that can be used in place of any other card. If, for example, twos or jokers were wild, a two or a joker could be used to make up a higher ranking hand (see Figure 4.2).

The use of wild cards is common in private games. However, they drastically change the odds so you need to completely re-think the way you play the game.

Where wild cards are used, the higher ranking hands are much easier to achieve. Without wild cards, there are only four ways in which a royal flush can be made. By having, for example, twos wild, the number of ways a royal flush can be made hugely increases to 504. The odds of being dealt a royal flush are cut from 649,739/1 to 5156/1. All of the other hands are also more easily achieved. What may have been a good hand in a game without wild cards may be a poor hand if wild cards are used.

the two is used
to give three of
a kind

the two completes
a full house

two twos
complete a royal
flush

the joker
completes a
flush

the joker makes
five of a kind

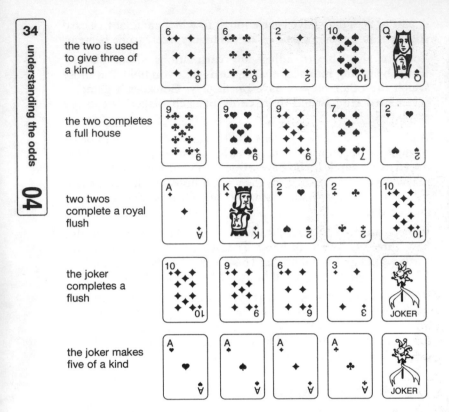

figure 4.2 using wild cards

Instead of nominating one of the values already in use as wild, the jokers may be added to the pack and made wild. This will completely change the calculations again, as more cards are used. If three jokers are added, the number of possible five card poker hands increases to 3,478,761. The number of ways a royal flush can be made will be 224 compared to 504 if the twos were wild. The odds against a royal flush will be increased to 15,529/1.

In this chapter you will learn:
- how to bet
- betting strategies
- what happens if a player runs out of money

Developing a betting strategy

You need to develop a betting strategy that will maximize your winnings whilst minimizing your losses. Your betting strategy also needs to be varied so that the other players can't predict your hand. If you always double the stakes when you have a good hand it will soon be noted by the other players. Players who always bet the minimum possible will immediately advertise their good hand if they suddenly place a huge bet.

From your player profiles you will have a good indication of your opponents' reactions to particular levels of betting. Some players may back down after a modest raise, while others may need a huge raise in order to fold. You will be able to spot the players who are staying in the game simply because it is not costing them very much. Your profile may tell you that one particular player always folds early on when he has nothing. If he is still there in the later rounds of betting, you will know to treat him with caution.

When to raise

The way you bet throughout the game can determine whether you win or lose. See Figure 5.1. Suppose you are playing seven card stud. Your two hole cards (the cards that are dealt face down) are a pair of jacks (Player A). The manner in which you bet early on could be enough to win you the game. If, after the third card is dealt, you make a big raise, you may force players to fold who could potentially beat you. After the first three cards, Player B has a poor hand. He would be likely to fold if the stakes were suddenly increased.

However, the situation may be entirely different if you do not raise. Player B may continue playing, simply because it is not costing him very much. He still has the possibility of being dealt another queen. If his fourth card is a queen, he is then in a stronger position. If he then raises after this card, you are in trouble, as you know you do not have enough to beat a pair of queens.

Another situation may arise if you have an exceptionally good hand such as a full house. You want to keep the other players betting for as long as possible to maximize the pot. Large bets early on will just increase the chance of everyone folding. If everyone folds, you only succeed in winning the ante. By placing smaller bets and gradually increasing them you can try to keep more players betting for longer. Your knowledge of the players will determine just how far you can raise the stakes without making them fold.

A
hole cards

B
hole cards

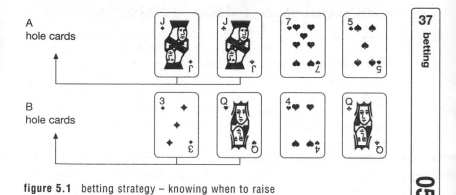

figure 5.1 betting strategy – knowing when to raise

Bluffing

Just because your hand is poor it doesn't automatically mean you will lose. Having the nerve to bluff and back up the bluff with a heavy round of betting can cause other players to fold, even when their hands are better than yours. Do not expect to win every hand that you play. Bluffing should be used sparingly. If you bluff too often it can work against you. There will be situations where you have a fairly good hand but want to force out a player who you suspect may have a slightly better hand. If you are known as a player who bluffs a lot, your strategy may not work. No matter how much you raise, your opponent will not back down. If, instead, you are known as a player who rarely bluffs, a large raise by you will be taken much more seriously.

Knowing when to fold

Don't stay in the game for too long. If your hand isn't good enough to win, withdraw from the game. By continually staying in for one extra round of betting with a hand that is clearly going to get beaten, you lose more money than you need to. If you are bluffing and the bluff is obviously not working, then fold. It is pointless to keep raising.

Playing in casinos

A sign will indicate the minimum and maximum bets for each table. Before any cards are dealt each player makes a bet called the ante. Players have the option of betting the same amount as the previous player, raising the bet, checking (reserving the right to bet in the next round) or folding. Some games allow players to bet blind. Whatever you decide to do, you must make your intentions clear. To stay in the game you need to bet at least as much as the previous player.

Playing in private games

Private games offer a great deal of flexibility as players can organize the betting in a wide range of ways. It is best to keep to a fairly simple method of betting. If you use a complicated system it can interfere with the game. You have enough to think about without having to perform complex calculations just to determine your next bet.

Whatever system you use, you should always agree a minimum and maximum bet, and the amount of the ante. It is often a good idea to include an ante. This ensures that there is initially some money in the pot which may give the players the incentive to try to win it. Games which do not specify an ante can be slow to develop.

Instead of each player contributing an ante-bet, you may encounter games where the dealer contributes a number of chips to the pot. As each player takes turns in being the dealer, the amount each player contributes evens out over the course of a session.

Using a set limit

With this system, players agree both a minimum and a maximum bet. The range between the minimum and maximum should be fairly wide to give players the opportunity of making decent raises. If, for example, the gap between the minimum and maximum bet is only four chips, it does not give a player much opportunity to force other players to fold. Players will tend to stay in the game simply because it is not costing them very much. If you have a range of around ten chips, a high raise will have more impact. Someone raising the stake by ten chips will be able to force players into folding.

In the example that follows an ante of one chip has been agreed which means that each player must bet one chip before any cards are dealt. To stay in the game each player must bet an amount equal to the previous player. They can also raise the stakes by betting an additional amount up to the maximum bet.

Example of betting using a set limit

Minimum bet – 1 chip; maximum bet – 10 chips; ante – 1 chip
Four players – A, B, C and D

Player	Action taken	Stake	Total in the pot
A, B, C & D	Ante	1 chip from each player	4
A	bets 2 chips	2	6
B	raises 2 chips	4	10
C	bets 4 chips	4	14
D	folds	0	14
A	raises 2 chips	6	20
B	raises 5 chips	11 *	31
C	folds	0	31
A	raises 2 chips	13	44
B	raises 10 chips	23 **	67
A	folds	0	67

Player B wins the pot of 67 chips. His stake was 39 chips.
Net winnings: 67 – 39 = 28 chips.

* Although the maximum bet is 10 chips, this is not the maximum number of chips that a player stakes. Player B's bet consists of a bet of 6 chips to match the previous bet, plus 5 chips which is his own bet.
** Player B matches the previous bet of 13 chips and makes an additional bet of 10 chips.

Straddle method

In this method of betting, the first player makes a bet called the ante. The second player makes a bet of double the ante called the straddle. The cards are dealt. After looking at his cards the third player has two choices. He can either make a bet of double the straddle or withdraw from the game. The other players then take turns to decide whether or not to bet or withdraw from the game. To stay in the game, each player must bet at least the same amount as the previous player. Bets can also be increased, usually up to an agreed maximum. Betting will continue until no one else raises or the maximum bet is reached. The players then reveal their hands.

Example of the straddle method

Ante – 2 chips; maximum bet – 20 chips; opening bet double last straddle

Four players – A, B, C and D

Player	Action	Stake	Total in pot
A	makes ante-bet	2 chips	2
B	doubles ante	4 chips	6
C	opens	8 chips	14
D	calls	8 chips	22
A	folds	0	22
B	raises 5	13 chips	35
C	calls	13 chips	48
D	folds	0	48
B	raises 10	23 chips	71
C	folds	0	71

Player B wins the pot of 71 chips. His stake was 40 chips.

Net winnings: 71 – 40 = 31 chips.

Freeze out

With this method of betting, each player has an equal amount of capital at the beginning of the game. The object is for one player to win all the chips. Betting is arranged using any agreed method. When a player runs out of chips, there is an immediate showdown and the player with the highest ranking hand wins the pot.

Running out of money

Occasionally a player may run out of money midway through a game. In this situation a second pot may be opened. The remaining players make all further bets to the second pot. The player with insufficient funds waits until either one player remains or there is a showdown. If one player remains, he wins the second pot. If several players remain, then the one with the highest ranking hand takes the second pot. The hand that won the second pot is then compared to that of the player who has run out of money. The player with the highest ranking hand wins the original pot.

06
cheating

In this chapter you will learn:
- how players cheat
- how to combat cheating
- shuffling the cards

Poker is particularly vulnerable to cheating. There are lots of ways in which players can be duped. Playing in legal casinos is the safest way to ensure that the games are played fairly. If you play in private games, you should be aware of the many methods of cheating so that you can ensure that you are not conned.

Betting light

One of the easiest ways to cheat is for players to not fully contribute to the pot. If there are a lot of chips already in the pot, it is not always obvious how many chips a particular player is adding. You may see him pick up the required number of chips, but it is very easy to just drop a few into the pot and palm the rest. Everyone's attention then switches to the next player and the one who palmed the chips is able to discreetly put them back on the table with his own chips.

Alternatively, a cheat may bet so quickly that you do not see what chips he picks up. The only indication that you get of a bet being made is the clinking of chips as more are added.

Marked cards

In poker it is advantageous for gamblers to know what cards the other players are holding. Anyone with this knowledge is able to bet only when he knows he has a winning hand.

The easiest way to accomplish this is to mark the backs of the cards in such a way so that they can be 'read' by the cheat. The designs on the backs of the cards are often intricate patterns. It is possible to add shading, small dots or to slightly thicken lines. These changes will not be noticed by the other players unless the cards are carefully scrutinized.

Even if someone produces a sealed pack of cards, they may still be marked. It is a relatively simple task to mark the cards and reseal them in their original packing. Professionally marked cards can also be purchased. The designs may be identical but certain cards may have a slightly thicker border on one side.

Before you begin playing you should carefully study the cards. Pay particular attention to the corners. Marks are placed here so that they can be seen when players are holding their cards. Compare the high cards to the low cards. Often only the high cards will be marked.

check differences in pattern design

check for creases on the corners of cards

figure 6.1 cheating using marked cards

Cards should also be checked during the course of play as they can become marked either intentionally or accidentally. Most commonly corners of cards can be bent to make creases visible. If any marks are found use a new pack of cards.

Technicians

Dealers can cheat in lots of ways. Someone who is skilled at manipulating the cards is called a technician. It is easy to look at the bottom card whilst shuffling. With practice it is possible to position desired cards at the bottom of the pack. The dealer can then deal his hand from the bottom of the deck and the other players' hands from the top.

Another method is to spot a good card whilst shuffling and to place it on the top of the deck. The dealer saves this card for himself and deals from the second card down to the other players.

A player can also use a spiked ring to make an indentation in the cards. When it is his turn to deal, he simply has to feel the cards to identify the best ones. He can either save them for himself using one of the techniques already described or simply keep track of which player receives them.

Cutting the cards

To combat cheating by the dealer it is common practice for one of the players to cut the cards. However, the dealer can overcome the problem of the cards being cut by bending one card in the middle so that it is slightly curved. The cards will tend to be cut at the curved card. Try this yourself with a pack of cards – you will find that you easily grip the curved card but the ones below it slip through your fingers. A dealer cannot guarantee that it will work every time but on the occasions when it does, he is guaranteed of a win.

A One card is bent along the middle of its longest side

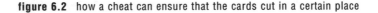

B The bent card is placed in the desired position in the pack

C You easily grip the bent card

figure 6.2 how a cheat can ensure that the cards cut in a certain place

Collusion

With poker, the game relies on players not knowing each other's hands. If two or more people are colluding, they can ensure that their best hand is always played. The player with the poorer hand will simply drop out of the betting.

The colluding players will have a set of signals to tell the other player their hand. This could be anything from the position that chips are placed in, the lighting of a cigarette or the scratching of an ear.

Combating cheating

If you play in private games, be particularly wary of playing cards with strangers. Obviously you should not play in rooms with mirrors, but other reflective surfaces can allow a cheat to find out what cards players are holding. With the correct lighting, it is very easy to see what cards are being dealt to players if a table has a highly polished glass or marble surface. You should always, therefore, play on a table covered in felt or a cloth. Also check the light fittings, some glass lampshades act as excellent mirrors.

Always insist on checking the cards for marks before and after play. Watch the dealer carefully. Does he hold the cards in an unusual way. Someone dealing the second or bottom card is likely to cover the cards with his hands. Always cut the cards by inserting a card not in play, like a joker. This gets round the problem of someone bending one of the cards. Keep track of how much money goes into the pot. Carefully watch other players when they make their bets. Make sure they add the number of chips required. If you suspect other players of cheating, stop playing.

Burning of cards

Another way to try to combat cheating by the dealer is for several cards to be 'burnt'. The top five cards of a deck are removed and not used in play. However, a skilled technician can still shuffle the cards in such a way that his desired hand will be achieved.

To ensure fair play it is best to play card games in legal casinos. Here, new cards are used each day, and they are checked for marks before and after use. If cards do become marked during the course of play, they will be exchanged for new cards. The dealer controls all the betting and will ensure that the players contribute the correct number of chips. Cameras are installed on all the tables to record the action, so if you suspect either a player or the dealer of cheating, there is a record of the game which can be studied.

Shuffling and dealing the cards

To ensure the cards are really well mixed, it is best to use a combination of methods for shuffling. Laying the cards face down on the table and giving them a good mix is a good method of shuffling. This should be combined with a riffle shuffle. Here, the pack is split into two and your thumbs are used to riffle the cards so that the two halves are combined (see Figure 6.3).

The over hand style of shuffling where a number of cards are picked up from the back of the pack and dropped a few cards at a time to the front of the pack is most open to abuse as a technician can arrange the cards into virtually any desired order.

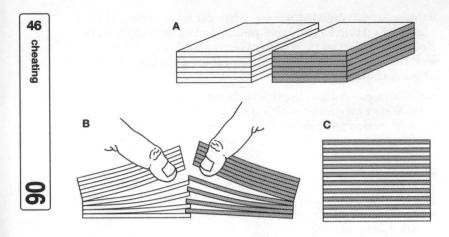

figure 6.3 the riffle shuffle

Invite a player to cut the cards. Ensure that none of the cards is exposed when you deal. Take particular care that the bottom card cannot be seen by any of the players. Angle the cards down towards the table when you deal. Take care not to reveal cards that have been discarded.

It is very important that players do not see either the card on the bottom of the pack or any discarded cards. If a player does see other cards he can use that information to his advantage. Suppose you see that the card on the bottom of the pack is a king. If you are dealt a pair of queens, you already know that the odds of being beaten by a pair of kings is reduced.

07

the different games of poker

Five card draw

Each player receives five cards face down and after an initial round of betting has an opportunity to exchange any card in his hand for new cards from the deck. It is usual to select the cards that are being discarded and to return them to the dealer before new cards are drawn.

What hands should you play?

There is little point in staying in with anything lower than a high pair. A high pair may be enough to win without any improvement. If, for example, you stay in with a pair of sixes and take three cards in an attempt to get three of a kind, the odds against you achieving your desired hand are 7.5/1. Your opponent may have a pair of jacks and also has the same chance as you of improving. However, if neither of you improves he has already beaten your hand. If you still decide to stay in the game, you need to convince him that you got the desired cards on the draw. Your early bets may have given him no cause for concern. In order to be convincing you will need to make a big raise to force him out. If your bluff fails it may be costly.

You should be able to gain a fair indication of the types of hands held from the number of cards that each player exchanges. Also, if you compare the odds of being dealt a good hand in the first deal to the odds of improving on cards already held (see table opposite), you can see that the odds of improving are much better than the odds of having a good initial hand. So, if in the first deal you have nothing, it is better to withdraw from the game instead of exchanging all five cards. Even exchanging four cards needs something short of a miracle to give you a good hand. You will be betting against players who may already hold good cards and who, by exchanging one or two, can also improve.

Holding a pair

If you are holding a pair, you can improve your hand by exchanging up to three cards. However, if you exchange three cards, the other players will be immediately aware that you are likely to have a pair. Anyone with two pair or three of a kind will be confident that he has a better hand.

Instead of drawing three cards, you have the option of keeping a kicker. The 'kicker' will usually be your highest other card. Instead of exchanging three cards, you exchange two. Your chances of improving your hand are slightly reduced, but now

Odds against improving hands in draw poker

Hand held	Cards drawn	Desired hand	Odds against achieving hand
Three of a kind	2	any improvement	17/2
Three of a kind + kicker	1	any improvement	11/1
Three of a kind	1	full house	15/1
Three of a kind	1	four of a kind	46/1
Three of a kind	2	full house	15/1
Three of a kind	2	four of a kind	23/1
Two pair	1	full house	11/1
One pair	3	three of a kind	7.5/1
One pair	3	full house	97/1
One pair	3	four of a kind	359/1
One pair + kicker	2	any improvement	3/1
One pair + kicker	2	two pair using kicker	7.5/1
One pair + kicker	2	two pair without kicker	17/1
One pair + kicker	2	three of a kind	12/1
One pair + kicker	2	full house	119/1
One pair + kicker	2	fours	1080/1
Four card flush	1	pair	3/1
Four card flush	1	flush	4.5/1
Four card incomplete straight flush (open ended)	1	straight or flush	2/1
		straight flush	22.5/1
Incomplete straight	1	any improvement	1/1
Flush (inside)		pair	3/1
		flush	5/1
		straight	11/1
		straight flush	46/1

the other players will be unsure as to whether you only have a pair or a possible three of a kind.

However, do not fall into the pattern of always retaining a kicker when you have a pair as the other players will soon work out your strategy. Vary your play as much as possible so that your opponents are never sure about your hand.

You may decide that the time is right to pull off a bluff. You may decide to take just one card to give an indication of a possible two pair that you are trying to improve to a full house or a possible flush. A big raise after drawing cards would be needed to back up the bluff.

Alternatively, you may decide to take no cards. The players will be aware that you may have been dealt a very good hand, but again, they cannot be certain. They will be aware of the odds against you obtaining a high ranking hand with just five cards, but if you are known as a player who rarely bluffs then you may be successful. However, if you have bluffed too often in the past, you are unlikely to get away with another bluff.

Holding three of a kind

You have the choice of exchanging either one or both cards. You have a greater chance of improving to a full house or four of a kind by taking two cards. However, if you always take two cards you will alert the other players to the fact that you are likely to have three of a kind. If, instead, you occasionally exchange one card, keeping a kicker, you will keep the other players guessing.

Holding a full house

It is pointless trying to improve to four of a kind. You already hold a hand which is going to be very difficult for other players to beat, and so your real decision should be whether to raise before the draw to force out other players who may improve on the draw.

Example game

Figure 7.1 shows the hands of four players before and after the draw.

Player A has been dealt a good initial hand with a pair of kings. Three cards are drawn. He fails to get three of a kind but gets another pair. The fifth card is an ace. He knows that even if another player has a pair of aces, the fact that he is holding an ace makes it harder for him to achieve three of a kind.

Player B has a poor initial hand so decides to fold.

Player C has two pair. Although the cards are low, he has the opportunity of making a full house by drawing one card. He has seen player A draw three cards, so he knows that A's initial hand is a pair. He fails to improve his hand.

original hand   after the draw

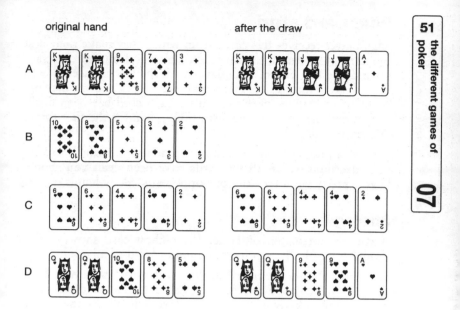

figure 7.1 example of draw poker hands

Player D has a high pair of two queens. He is aware that A also initially had a pair. Player C only took one card so he is possibly going for a full house, a flush, a straight, or is bluffing. D draws three cards and improves to two pair.

Player A raises. Player C decides to fold. He realizes that player A may have improved, possibly to three of a kind or two pair. Although player C has two pair, they are low value cards.

Player D knows he has a fairly good hand so he raises player A. He knows two pair with kings or aces could beat him but he holds an ace so knows the chances of player A holding a pair of aces or three aces is reduced.

The game now becomes a test of nerves between A and D. If either backs down then the other will win the pot. If the game continues to a showdown then player A will win the showdown.

Five card stud

Each player receives five cards from which they make their best five card poker hand. Initially each player is dealt one card face up and one face down. The player with the lowest face-up card must make a forced bet. The remaining cards are dealt face up. A round of betting takes place after each card has been dealt. The player showing the highest ranking hand is the first to bet in each round.

Here you progressively get more information on which to base your decisions. Once all the cards have been dealt you should have a pretty good idea of your opponents' likely hands.

Strategy

If you cannot match or better the highest card showing you should fold. Ideally aim for a minimum hand of a high pair.

See Figure 7.2. In the initial deal, player B has the lowest face-up card so makes a forced bet. As each card is dealt more information is known about each player's hand. By the fourth card players A, C and D are all showing pairs. Player B has the potential to achieve a straight flush.

By the time the fifth card has been dealt, it is clear what the possible hands might be. The best hands are A – three of a kind with eights, B – a straight flush, C – three of a kind with sevens, and D – four of a kind with sixes. If each player achieves his best possible hand then player B would win on a showdown.

Each player needs to assess their chances of winning against the other hands.

If player A has another 8, he is certain of beating player C. He also knows that if B has any card other than a diamond then his hand is nothing. If player D's hole card (the card dealt face down) is not a 6 or an ace then player A will also beat him. One of the aces is revealed in player C's hand, which gives D less chance of achieving a full house.

Player B knows that he has potentially the best hand. If his hole card is not a diamond then whether or not he wins will depend on how well he can bluff.

If player C has another 7, he will have to decide whether or not the other players are bluffing. Although all the players have the potential for good hands it is unlikely that they have all achieved them. If the other players are all bluffing, player C would win a showdown.

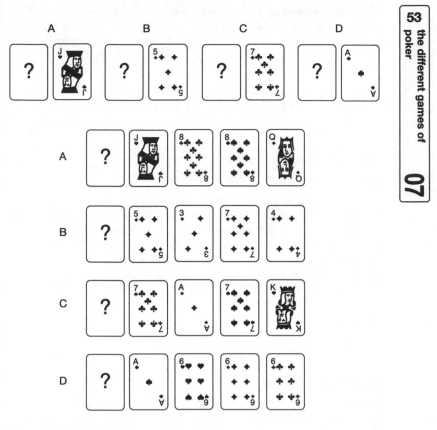

figure 7.2 examples of five card stud hands

Seven card stud

Seven card stud is the one of the most popular forms of poker. Each player receives seven cards. The aim is to make the best possible five card poker hand from the seven cards dealt to you. The player with the best hand wins all the money staked, less the rake (a charge made by the casino for the use of its facilities).

Initially three cards are dealt, two face down and one face up. The fourth, fifth and sixth cards are dealt face up, and the seventh face down. You therefore have four cards on display to the other players and three cards which are hidden from view.

There is a round of betting after each card has been dealt. The person with the highest ranking poker hand on view is the first to either bet or fold in each round of betting. So, someone with three of a kind would be the first to bet if all the other players are showing one pair.

Here, you have quite a lot of useful information on which to base your strategy. You may be able to deduce from the other players' four cards on display that your hand has no chance of winning. You can use your knowledge of the odds to calculate your opponents' chance of completing hands that are shown. However, the other players can also deduce the same amount of information from your cards on view.

If your cards on display show the potential for a good hand which could beat the likely hands of all the other players, but you do not hold the cards necessary, you have the option to bluff. By continually raising the stakes you may force the other players to fold. The game then becomes a test of nerves. The other players will realize what your potential hand is and will see that you are betting heavily. They will then have to decide whether or not you are bluffing. If you force all the other players to fold, your hand will not be revealed and they will never know that you were bluffing. If, however, a showdown is reached, your cards will be revealed.

Example hands

See Figure 7.3. Suppose you are player A. You have two pair. You can immediately see that player B has a better hand with three of a kind. Player C also has two pair which beats your hand, but could have a full house if he has either another king or another five. In the cards that you are showing, you have the 9, 8 and 7 of hearts. Although your hand can't win in a showdown against either A or B, by using a heavy round of betting you could convince them that you have the other two cards necessary to complete a straight flush.

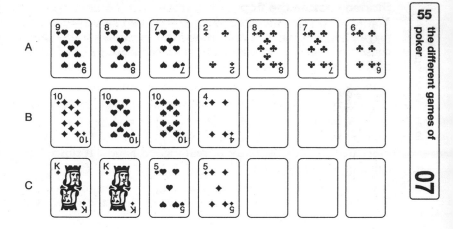

Figure 7.3 examples of seven card stud hands

Hold 'em

Each player receives two cards face down. Five cards are then placed face up in the centre of the table, and these cards are used by all the players. Each player uses any combination of the two cards in his hand and the five community cards to make the best five card poker hand.

The deal

Initially each player receives his two hidden cards followed by a round of betting. Players often have the opportunity to bet blind (to place a bet before they look at their cards). This helps to increase the pot. Three of the community cards are then dealt, called the 'flop'. Another round of betting follows. A further community card is dealt followed by a round of betting, then the final community card is dealt.

Since each player's cards are hidden from view, the only indication you have of their possible hands is the way in which they are betting. In order to make a proper assessment, you really need to see all of the community cards first. Once you have seen these, you are then in a better position to assess the likely hands.

Strategy before the flop

You need to decide whether or not your two cards are worth playing. In general terms it is worthwhile playing any pair, consecutive cards of the same suit, such as 9, 8 or 6, 5 and fairly high cards of the same suit, such as J, 9.

Strategy after the flop

You now have a better indication of the possible hands. You can assess your position against all the other possibilities. If the community cards have not helped you, they may well have given other players the possibility of really good hands. If this is the situation then fold now.

If you are still in a fairly good position, you need to force out anyone who can beat you either now or once the other two cards have been dealt.

A community cards   player's cards

B community cards   player's cards

figure 7.4 'nuts'

Nuts

Occasionally a situation may arise where you know that you have the best possible hand (nuts) that can be made using the community cards. There is no way that you can be beaten. Clearly in this situation you want to maximize the pot. Your strategy for betting will need to be based on your knowledge of the players. You need to keep the betting at the right level to keep as many of the players betting as possible (see Figure 7.4).

Example hands

See Figure 7.5. The best possible hand from the community cards is four of a kind, followed by a full house then three of a kind.

Player A will deduce that he has a good hand with three of a kind. He knows that he has the best possible three of a kind and can only be beaten by a full house and since he holds one of the aces, the chances of anyone holding either two queens, two fours or two threes are low.

However, player B has a full house. He knows that only four of a kind or a full house with queens or fours could beat him.

Player C has nothing and would be wise to fold. Betting would then commence between A and B. It would probably develop into a test of nerves to determine who would fold, or alternatively would ultimately lead to a showdown which B would win.

community cards

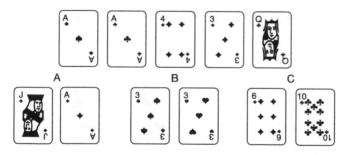

figure 7.5 example of hold 'em hands

Omaha

Each player receives four cards face down. Five cards are then placed face up in the centre of the table to be used by all the players. Each player uses any combination of two cards in his hand and three community cards to make the best five card poker hand.

The game is dealt in a similar way to hold 'em with a flop of three cards. You may also be given the opportunity to bet blind (to bet before looking at your cards). What makes the game more complicated is the way in which the five card poker hand is made. When you see the cards you need to give some thought as to what hand you have actually got. At first glance you may seem to have an exceptionally good hand. But you need to remember that you can only use two of the cards in your hand (see Figure 7.6).

By looking at the cards in total, player A can immediately see a full house (three fours and two tens). However, because only two cards can be used from his hand he only has two pair (two tens and two fours).

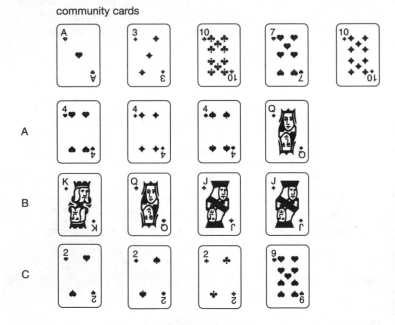

figure 7.6 example of omaha hands

Player B appears to have a straight (A, K, Q, J, 10) but the hand actually held is two pair (two jacks and two tens).

At first glance player C may appear to have a full house (three twos and two tens). However, he can only use two cards from his hand so only holds two pairs (two tens and two twos).

From the community cards, you can obtain a lot of information about the possible hands held by other players. In Figure 7.6, the possible hands are: four of a kind – one player has the other two tens; a full house – one player has one ten and an ace, seven or three or holds two of the other aces, sevens or threes; three of a kind – one of the other tens, or a pair of aces, sevens or threes; two pair – a player holds another pair or one ace, seven or two.

Strategy

The strategy is similar to hold 'em. You really need to see the flop before you can make any decision. However, a situation can arise when it is wise to fold immediately after you have been dealt your hole cards.

Being dealt four of a kind in your hole cards is one of the worst possible situations. You can only use two cards so at best you have a pair with no chance of improving on them. Being dealt three of a kind also gives you only a remote chance that the fourth card will appear in the community cards. The same is true of being dealt four cards to a possible flush; your chances of making the flush are drastically reduced.

figure 7.7 hands to fold on in omaha

The best cards to play with are high pairs or high cards of the same suit (if you hold only two of the same suit) which could lead to a flush.

After the flop, you will be in a much better position to judge your chances of winning. Then you can assess all of the possibilities and work out your chances of making a good hand. It is at this stage that you need to force out anyone who has the potential to improve his or her hand into one that could beat yours.

Nuts

As with hold 'em, occasionally a situation may arise where you know that you have the best possible hand (nuts) that can be made using the community cards. There is no way that you can be beaten. Clearly in this situation you want to maximize the pot. Your strategy for betting will need to be based on your knowledge of the players. You need to keep betting at the right level to keep as many of the players betting as possible.

Caribbean stud poker

The games we have looked at so far all involve betting against the other players – you have to beat everyone else playing in order to win the pot. Caribbean stud poker differs because it is a banking game. Instead of playing against other players you are playing against the casino which acts as a bank, paying out all winning bets. The casino provides a dealer. In order to win, you have only to beat the dealer's hand. The other players' hands do not affect the outcome of your bets.

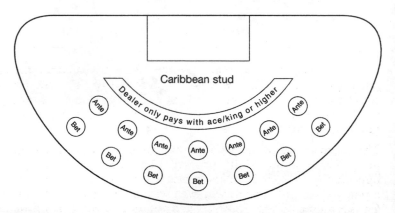

figure 7.8 Caribbean stud layout

The game

The object of the game is to win by having a five card poker hand that ranks higher than the dealer's. Each player makes an ante-bet and is dealt five cards face down. The dealer receives four cards face down and one card face up.

Players then look at their cards and have the option to play or fold. If a player folds, his ante-bet is lost. If a player decides to continue, he must then make a further bet of double his ante-bet.

The dealer will then reveal his hand. He must have an ace and a king or higher in order to play his hand. If a player's hand beats the dealer's, the ante-bet is paid at evens. See the table below for the odds for the second bet. If the dealer does not have at least an ace and a king then a player is paid even money on the ante-bet and the additional bet is void (not lost). If, however, the dealer's hand beats the player's, then both bets are lost.

Payout odds for an additional bet in Caribbean stud poker	
One pair or less	1/1 (even)
Two pair	2/1
Three of a kind	3/1
Straight	4/1
Flush	5/1
Full house	7/1
Four of a kind	20/1
Straight flush	50/1
Royal flush	100/1

If the dealer and the player play the same poker hand, the remaining cards are taken into consideration. If all five cards are equal, the hand is void (the bet is not lost). Neither the ante-bet or the additional bet are paid. The type of suit makes no difference to the hand.

The disadvantage of this game is that you are relying purely on luck. There is no skill involved. You do not have the opportunity to bluff. In poker games where you are playing for a pot, you are still able to win even with a poor hand but with Caribbean stud poker, if you have a poor hand, you stand little chance of winning.

The minimum odds in this game are evens. In a normal game of poker with, for example, seven players you would have odds of at least 6/1 and quite often a great deal better.

The odds paid for the additional bet are also poor compared to the chances of achieving them. Odds of 100/1 are paid for a royal flush, yet your chances of being dealt one are 649,739/1. The only advantage you have is that you know how much each game is going to cost you.

Caribbean stud poker should be played only for amusement purposes. If you want to win money, you are better off playing games where you are contesting for a pot.

Pai gow poker

In pai gow poker each player in turn has the option of being banker. The game is a mixture of the Chinese game pai gow and American poker. It is played with one deck of 52 cards, plus one joker. The joker can be used only as an ace, or to complete a straight, a flush, a straight flush, or a royal flush.

The casino provides the dealer. Each player is dealt seven cards. The cards are arranged to make two hands; a two card hand and a five card hand. The five card hand must rank higher or be equal to the two card hand (see table of rankings below).

The object of the game is for both of your hands to rank higher than both of your opponent's hands. Your two card hand must rank higher than your opponent's two card hand and your five card hand must rank higher than your opponent's five card hand.

Ranking of hands in pai gow poker

Five card hand	Two card hand
Five aces (five aces plus the joker)	One pair
Royal flush	High card
Straight flush	
Four of a kind	
Full house	
Flush	
Straight	
Three of a kind	
Two pair	
One pair	
High card	

If one of your hands ranks the same as your opponent's hand, this is a tie (or copy hand). The banker wins all ties. If you win one hand but lose the other, this is known as a 'push'. In push hands no money is exchanged. Winning hands are paid even money less a five per cent commission. Losing hands lose the money bet.

The game

The dealer and each player in turn are all given the opportunity to be banker. You can only be banker if you bet against the dealer the last time he was banker. You need to have sufficient chips to pay the bets should your opponent win.

You arrange your cards into the two hands and place them face down on the table. Once you've put them down, you can no longer touch them. The dealer will turn over his cards and make his hands. Each hand is compared to the dealer's hands. If the player wins one hand and loses the other, the bet is void (a push). If you wrongly set your hand – you lose.

The major disadvantage to this game is that you are relying on the luck of the deal – there is no skill involved. If your cards are poor, there is no opportunity to bluff. The dealer plays his hand if he has the minimum required and does not drop out of the betting.

As with Caribbean stud poker, the odds are also poor compared to playing with a pot.

See Figure 7.9. Player A has beaten the dealer's five card hand but has failed to beat the two card hand. This is a push – the money bet is not lost.

Player B has beaten both hands. His bet is paid at even money less five per cent commission.

Player C has failed to beat the dealer's five and two card hand. He loses his bet.

dealer's hands

player's hands

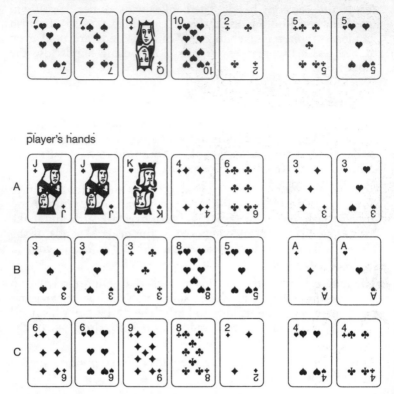

figure 7.9 examples of pai gow poker hands

08 playing in a casino

In this chapter you will learn:
- how playing in a casino differs from private games
- how play is organised
- card room etiquette

Casinos are purpose-built gaming establishments, which offer facilities for playing a wide range of gambling games including various forms of poker. Casinos are legal in many countries and are often state controlled or legislated. They tend to be located in resorts and large population areas. Local gaming laws determine when they may open. There are casinos in many countries around the world where poker can be played including Great Britain, the United States of America, Canada, continental Europe, South Africa and Australia. Some casinos also give lessons in the games. These allow players to practise without risking any money. Casinos also host poker tournaments (see Chapter 9).

British casinos

Great Britain has over 120 casinos. They tend to be found in large towns and cities and in tourist areas. There are over 20 in London. More than 40 casinos have facilities for playing poker.

British casinos are strictly controlled by the Gaming Board who issue licences for premises and casino staff. Checks are carried out to ensure that no gaming personnel or casino owners have criminal records. Daily opening hours are from 2 p.m. to 4 a.m.

All of the casinos are 'member only' clubs. In order to gamble you need to become a member or to be signed in by a member. You will be required to show two forms of identification, one of which must be a major form of identification, such as a passport. After you have applied for membership, 24 hours must pass before you are allowed to gamble. Some casinos also charge a membership fee. If you are travelling from abroad and want to gamble, it is possible to apply for membership in advance.

Continental Europe

Most countries in continental Europe have casinos. They tend to be smaller, more intimate establishments than those found in the United States. Countries with casinos include Monaco, France, Germany, Austria, Spain, Greece, the Netherlands and Belgium. Poker is becoming more popular in Europe and is played in increasingly more casinos.

United States and Canada

Casino gaming is legal in most of the United States. The casinos are huge establishments and are often incorporated in larger leisure complexes. They are located in the traditional venues of Las Vegas and Atlantic City and also on Native American reservations. Most are open 24 hours a day. Over 260 casinos have facilities for poker.

In Canada there are government-owned casinos, 24 of which offer poker. Resort casinos are located in tourist areas. There are also provincial casinos, which attract locals.

The southern hemisphere

Australia has 14 casinos, which are privately operated under government-granted franchises. They are located in the major cities and Gold Coast resorts. Four casinos have facilities for poker. South Africa has recently granted gaming licenses for 40 casinos.

Selecting a casino

The amount you have budgeted to spend will largely determine the sort of casino you frequent. The minimum stakes for betting can vary quite considerably in different casinos. Generally, the more upmarket the club, the higher the stakes will be. You will therefore need to consider how many chips of the minimum stake your budget will purchase and how long they will last.

If you are playing for high stakes you will have more choice and can look for the best facilities. The more upmarket casinos provide private rooms for games. This facility allows high-staking customers to play in quieter surroundings. Instead of paying a percentage of the pot, you can often negotiate an hourly rate for this service.

What to expect

The casino provides all the facilities for playing poker including the gaming table, dealer and cards. There are set rules that determine how the game is dealt, how the betting is organized and what happens in the event of a dispute. A printed version of the rules is available on request.

Games played include Texas hold 'em, omaha, seven card stud and Caribbean stud poker. The games are played with casino chips, which can be purchased either on the table or from the cash point. When you leave the casino you simply hand in your chips at the cash point where they will be redeemed for money.

How does playing in a casino differ from private games?

- Casino poker is more formal.
- There is a limited choice of games.
- The dealer is employed by the casino and does not play in the game.
- Cheats are actively pursued and barred.
- The competitors you will be playing against will be strangers.

Why gamble in a casino?

The main incentive is to win money. The potential winnings are unlimited. This is because there is always a supply of players with large bankrolls. In many casinos it is also possible to play around the clock. There is always a game available. You will also gain more experience, as you will be playing against players of different abilities from beginners to professional gamblers.

One of the main advantages of playing in a casino is that you are guaranteed fairness. Chapter 6 describes some of the many ways of cheating at poker. In a casino there are lots of controls in place to make the games fair. The dealer is employed by the casino so has no interest in the game. This eliminates all the methods of cheating involved with dealing. New packs of cards are used and are constantly checked for marks. This rules out marked cards being used.

The casino staff allocate the seats, which makes it more difficult for colluding players to get on the same game. The winnings of players are monitored which makes it easy to identify colluding players. All games are videotaped and can be played back to identify cheats. If cheats are caught, they are barred from the casino. Their details are also given to other casinos, which makes it difficult for them to play elsewhere.

A casino is a safe environment with security staff, who will ensure that disputes are settled in a civil manner. You may win in a private game but could find yourself having to return your winnings to a player who threatens you with physical violence.

Costs

Playing in a casino is more expensive than in a private game. The casino makes a charge for the use of its services. In poker games this charge is in the form of a commission, which is usually a percentage of the pot. This charge is called the rake and is typically ten per cent of the pot. With Caribbean stud poker the charge is in the form of a house advantage. This means that winning bets are paid out at odds lower than the true chance of winning.

In some countries casino winnings are taxable. In the United States, for example, there is a 30 per cent tax on winnings. Non-resident aliens from some countries can apply for exemption. It is best to check the local legislation before betting as you could get a big shock when your tax bill arrives.

Some casinos also charge an entrance and membership fee.

Entry requirements

Some form of identification such as a passport or driving licence will often need to be shown as proof of identity and age. Some casinos may require you to enrol as a member. This will involve filling in a form with personal details such as name and address. The minimum age for gambling is often the age of majority but can be older. In the United States it is 21. In most other countries it is 18.

Many casinos have a dress code. Generally the more expensive establishments have stricter rules so it is advisable to wear smart dress. Often men are required to wear a jacket and tie.

You may be refused entry if you have been previously barred from a casino. This is because casinos share information about players caught cheating.

You are not allowed to take electronic items like computers, calculators or cameras on the gaming floor.

Subliminal practises

Casinos use a number of subliminal practises to keep you on the premises for longer and to encourage you to bet more. This includes gaming rooms where clocks and windows are absent, serving refreshments at the gaming tables and providing comps schemes. Comps is short for complimentary and refers to free refreshments, cigarettes, hotel rooms, flights and show tickets. A player's level of spending will determine which comps they receive. Many casinos operate a comp scheme where players can enrol to collect points towards comps. Players with large bankrolls are called high rollers or whales and receive all comps.

Chips are used instead of money. This makes it easy to get carried away and to bet more than you intended, as you do not associate the chip with its true value.

Stakes

For each game the stakes will be advertised. At peak times like weekends and holidays the minimum stakes may be raised. Players need to ensure that they have enough chips to last a game, as they are not usually allowed to purchase more chips until a game is completed. A game of draw poker requires around 40 times the minimum stake. Seven card stud requires around 50 times. Hold 'em and omaha need around 100 times.

Players who run out of chips during a game can still have a chance of winning a proportion of the pot. This is called the all-in rule. When a player runs out of chips, a second pot is started. The other players continue to play, contributing to the second pot. The winner of the game gets the second pot. The hand of the winner is then compared to that of the player who ran out of money. The player with the highest-ranking hand wins the first pot.

How play is organized

Poker is often played in a separate room, usually referred to as the card room. There will be a number of tables offering different games at different stake levels. Around eight to ten players can be seated at a table.

To start playing, you need to register for a game. If there is a seat free you will be able to start playing immediately. If all the seats are occupied, your name will be entered on a list and called out when a place becomes available.

Each table is operated by a casino dealer who is responsible for running the game. The dealer will shuffle and deal the cards, exchange money for chips, check that the players have bet the correct amount, place players' bets into the pot, remove losing hands, give change and pay the pot to the winner. The dealer also ensures the players are not cheating.

Tipping the dealer

Check local customs about tipping. In Great Britain it is illegal. In the United States and continental Europe it is customary though not obligatory to tip the dealer if you win the pot.

The size of the tip will depend on the amount won. On average tips are around one chip per pot won.

Card room etiquette

Each card room will have a set of rules about how players are expected to behave at the table. Most of the rules are designed to combat cheating.

The following is a general guide:

- Players may touch only their own cards and chips.
- All cards must remain in view at all times. They can't for example be held under the table or in a player's pocket.
- If a player drops a card or reveals one to another player, the hand is declared dead. The player will not be allowed to participate with the hand and any money contributed to the pot will be lost.
- Placing a chip on top of your cards shows you are still in the game.
- Chips must never be thrown.
- Bets must not be put directly into the pot. A bet is made by placing sufficient chips in front of you. The dealer checks that the amount is correct and adds them to the pot. This ensures that no one bets light.
- Players must give clear verbal instructions of their action. By calling out 'time' they will be granted extra time to make a decision.
- Players may stop playing when they like. They may also take breaks. If you intend to return to the game, you may leave your chips on the table. The dealer will ensure they are not touched. However, if you are absent for a long period, your seat may be allocated to another player.
- Don't put drinks directly on the gaming table as they disrupt the game if spilt. You will either be provided with a drinks holder or a separate table.

Fairness of the game

Strict controls are in place to ensure that players get a fair deal. In most countries government legislation and agencies ensure that games pay out a fair return to the players and that gaming equipment is fair. Casino staff, operators and premises are often licensed. Any infringement of gaming legislation can lead to their licence being withdrawn.

Gaming equipment is precision made and thoroughly checked before use. New packs of cards are used. At the beginning of gaming the playing cards are laid out on the table to show that full decks are being used. The cards are also scrutinized to check for any marks that could give players an unfair advantage. Any creased or marked cards are removed and replaced. While gaming is in progress the cards are continually scrutinized and any that become marked are removed and replaced. At the end of gaming the old cards are counted to ensure that none has been removed. They are then discarded.

The way that the cards are shuffled in a casino ensures that they are thoroughly mixed. A combination of methods is used including face down mixing, riffle shuffling and cutting of the cards. Usually a player is invited to insert a blank card into the pack to cut them.

As well as the dealer a number of other casino staff watch the games to ensure there is no cheating. An inspector checks the work of the dealer and is responsible for looking for cheats. The inspector also resolves any disputes that may arise. Since the games are recorded on videotape, disputes are easily settled. If you encounter a problem or suspect another player of cheating, ask the dealer to call the inspector. The pit boss is in charge of a group of tables and will often watch the games, again to ensure fair play. Security staff also carry out surveillance of players. Some wear uniforms and others are plain clothed and not obvious.

In addition to checking the videotapes of the game, the winning records of players can be analysed. Players who are consistently winning will be watched more closely for signs of cheating.

Casino records

Casinos keep records of how much players win and lose. They use this information to identify cheats and allocate comps. This information may also be passed to government agencies for the purposes of taxation and controlling money laundering. In the USA, for example, personal details of players winning large amounts are given to the IRS.

09

tournament play

A poker tournament is a competition between players for prizes. Competing in tournaments is an increasingly popular way to play poker. Each year more and more tournaments are being organized. They give players the opportunity to win a large prize for a relatively small entry fee. The more prestigious events attract players with greater skill and pay bigger prizes. For less experienced players there are lots of tournaments at lower stake levels.

Tournaments can be played at casinos, card rooms and on the internet. Casinos tend to hold tournaments at off-peak times. There are tournaments for all different types of poker games including hold 'em, seven card stud and omaha. Hold 'em is the most common tournament game as it was chosen to decide the champion in the World Series of Poker.

Tournaments allow players to test their skill against a large field of competitors. A minor tournament may have several hundred competitors. Major tournaments attract several thousand players. This gives players a great deal of experience. You will encounter competitors at various levels of skill ranging from hopeless to highly accomplished.

An advantage of tournaments is that they can work out a much cheaper way of playing than regular casino play, particularly in the minor tournaments. Assuming you get through the initial rounds, an entire day's play can cost the fraction of the price of a regular game. You know in advance how much it will cost. You also have a rough idea of the potential prizes.

Tournament play requires stamina and concentration. With conventional games you can take a break when you like and quit when you are ahead. With tournament play you are there for the duration, which can be up to 14 hours or more in one day. There are breaks allotted but they are short. A typical tournament will allow an hour for lunch and ten-minute breaks every one-and-a-half to two hours. In the World Series of Poker, for example, most events last two days. On the first day play starts at noon and continues until the competitors win their place for the final table. On the second day the finalists start playing at 4 p.m. and continue until one wins.

Types of tournament

There are two main types of tournament – freeze out or no-re-buy tournaments, and re-buy tournaments. In both types of games players are eliminated when they lose all of their chips.

Freeze out or no-re-buy tournaments

A freeze out tournament (no-re-buy) is where players receive an equal amount of chips at the start of the game. They play with this fixed amount of chips until the end of the game. If they get low on chips, they are not allowed to buy more. Players who lose all of their chips are eliminated. If there is a time limit, the winner is the player with the most chips at the end of the competition. In other tournaments play may continue until there is one winner at each table (all the other players have been eliminated). The winner then competes in the next round. Depending on the number of competitors there may be several rounds to eliminate players gradually. Breaks are allotted to allow players time to relax and eat. After each round of play seats are re-allocated for the next level. This may be by further draw or determined in advance, for example the finalists of table 1 may be scheduled to play the finalists of table 2.

Re-buy tournaments

In re-buy tournaments players are allowed to purchase extra chips at set points during the game. The amount of the re-buys is usually the same as the initial buy-in. In some tournaments re-buying of chips is unlimited. In others there are limits. The rules may stipulate, for example, that there are two further re-buys allowed. Play continues until players have no remaining chips or for a time limit where the player with the most chips is declared the winner.

Progressive stack re-buy tournaments

In progressive stack re-buy games the cost of the re-buy remains constant but the further you are into the re-buy period, the more chips you get. The effect of this is that the value of the chips decreases as the game continues.

Pot-limit and no-pot-limit

These are terms that refer to the size of the bets. A pot-limit is where the size of the bets may be any amount between that of the big blind and the total pot. The big blind is the minimum bet on the first round of betting. A no-pot limit means bets may be of any amount between the value of the big blind and the value of your remaining chips.

Costs

The costs for entering a tournament comprise the buy-in, re-buys and an entry fee. Minimum buy-ins start from around $15 to $20 and pay prizes of several hundred dollars. Buy-ins for major tournaments are as much as $10,000 with prizes of $1.5 million. The entry fee is kept by the casino to cover the cost of operating the tournament. An entry fee is typically ten per cent of the buy-in.

To find the overall cost of a tournament you will need to total the buy-in, cost of any re-buys and the entry fee. For example, a tournament advertised with a buy-in of $1000 and an entry fee of $100, will cost $1100 in total. A tournament advertised with a $500 buy-in and a $50 entry fee with two re-buys of $500 would cost a total of $1550 if you participate in all the buy-ins.

Entry requirements

Players are required to fill in a registration form and may be asked for proof of age and identity. Players must be over the minimum age to gamble. This varies depending on local gambling legislation. It is often the age of majority but can be older. Many tournaments are over subscribed so it is advisable to register early. At the registration, players pay the amount of the buy-in. If you intend to pay the buy-in by cheque, ensure you register early enough for the cheque to clear.

Some major tournaments have particular entry requirements. Players may be required to have won or have been placed in a major tournament. Alternatively a player may have to compete in a qualifying competition to gain entry. Most tournaments also have separate competitions for women players.

How play is organized

The tournament will be advertised giving the major conditions such as the amount of the buy-in, the value and number of re-buys and entry fee. A set of rules will be available. Play will be scheduled to take place over a certain amount of time. Some tournaments last for a few hours, others can be as long as several days.

A random draw is usually held to allocate seats. Players should take up their seats when directed to do so. It is advisable to arrive at least half an hour before play starts. If you do not arrive on time your seat may be allocated to another player or you may be disqualified.

The casino will supply a dealer who will control the game. The dealer will check initially that the correct players are seated at the table. The competition will start with an announcement of shuffle up and deal. The dealer will give the players their chips. Other casino staff will watch the game to ensure it is played fairly.

Each tournament will have its own set of rules. Commonly, players are not allowed to converse with each other or the spectators. Players must make all their own decisions and are not allowed to ask spectators or other players for advice. Players are not allowed to lend or borrow chips.

If a player runs out of chips during a hand, the all-in rule usually applies. This means that the players can still win the pot to which they have contributed. A second pot is then started for further bets.

The games will be closely watched for cheats who, if caught, will be disqualified. Games are usually videotaped and can be played back in the event of a dispute. The chances of players colluding are reduced as a random draw decides where players sit.

Prizes

At the end of play there will usually be a short ceremony to present the prizes. They are mostly paid out in cash. In some tournaments the prize can be the entry fee to enter a major competition (see Satellites). As well as the prize for the winner, there will often be prizes for several runners-up.

The prizes for most tournaments will depend on how many competitors there are. The value of all the buy-ins is totalled to give the prize money. In tournaments where re-buys are allowed, the value of the re-buys is also contributed to the prize money. The casino will often make a deduction for the rake. The majority of the prize fund is awarded to the winner. Several runners-up share the remainder. Some tournaments are winner takes all. In some tournaments there will be a guaranteed minimum prize. Often the prize will be more than the minimum.

In British tournaments the entire buy-in must be returned as prize money and no additional entry fee can be charged.

Satellites

A satellite is a poker tournament, which allows a player to win the stake to compete in a major tournament. For the major tournaments the minimum stake for the finale is high. For example, it may cost $10,000 to enter a tournament. A satellite may be organized for ten players with a $1000 buy-in. Play continues until there is one player only remaining. The winner receives all of the stake money, $10,000, which is enough to enter the main tournament.

For an even smaller stake, players can enter a super satellite. If they win it will also give them enough money to buy a seat in the major tournament. In super satellites there is more competition. Players may have to compete in several levels of play to win the stake for the major tournament. In the World Series of Poker, for example, there are super satellites costing $220, which give the players the opportunity of winning the $10,000 needed to enter the major competition.

Some major tournaments also organize satellites in different countries and on the internet. The prize will often include flights and hotel accommodation (see World Heads Up Poker Championship on page 80).

Major tournaments

The World Series of Poker

The World Series of Poker is the biggest and longest-running poker tournament in the world. It attracts the elite of poker players. It is held annually in May at Binion's Horseshoe Casino in Las Vegas. Across 30 days, a variety of tournaments are held. Most games take place over two days with play lasting for up to 14 hours in a day. Single table satellites are held 24 hours a day with buy-ins ranging from $170 to $1015. Super satellites start from $220. The action culminates in the no-limit Texas hold 'em tournament that takes place over four days. The entry fee is $10,000. The first prize is $1.5 million and membership of the Poker Hall of Fame. The finale is televised around the world.

The Jack Binion World Open

The Jack Binion World Open is modelled on the World Series of Poker. It takes place at Binion's Horseshoe and in Gold Strike casinos in Tunica. It is held annually in March and April. Buy-ins start from $330 rising to $5100 for the main competition, which is a no-limit Texas hold 'em tournament. Over 3000 competitors enter the tournament. Satellites and super satellites with buy-ins from $120 allow players to win their entrance fee for the main tournament.

Tournament of Champions of Poker

The Tournament of Champions of Poker, as the name suggests, is for players who have won major poker tournaments. Entry is also possible by winning a qualifying event. It is held in July at the Orleans Hotel in Las Vegas. It comprises $500 buy-in one-day tournaments with a top prize of over $1 million.

The European Championship

The European Championship is held at Casino Baden in Austria during October. The game played is seven card stud. Over 450 players from 23 countries compete for a prize of ATS 9 million, equivalent to over $550,000.

World Heads Up Poker Championship

This is held annually during May and June at the Concord Card Casino in Vienna, Austria. The casino has Europe's largest card room with 30 tables and a tournament room with 20 tables. Poker is played 24 hours a day. The main event is no-limit hold 'em with a Euro 640,000 purse. A seat in the main draw costs $2,125. The winner's prize is Euro 250,000. Satellites are played in card rooms throughout Europe, USA and Australia. It is also possible to play satellites on the internet. Winners of satellites get a seat in the championship, a flight and hotel accommodation.

The World Series of Poker Trial

During March the World Series of Poker Trial is held at the Concord Card Casino in Vienna, Austria. It duplicates the World Series of Poker held in Las Vegas with a no-limit Texas hold 'em competition which lasts four days.

The Poker Million Tournament

The Poker Million Tournament is held at Ladbrokes's Hilton Casino on the Isle of Man, Great Britain. It takes place during November. Players compete for a prize of £1.5 million.

Aussie Millions

The Aussie Millions is a new tournament that began in January 2003. It is held at the Crown Casino in Melbourne, Australia. It is a winner takes all no-limit hold 'em tournament with an expected purse of AS$1.5 million, and a first prize of AS$500,000.

Playing tips

If you are used to playing in private games, familiarize yourself with casino play. This may differ enormously from the games you are used to playing. Private games tend to be played with wild cards and hands that are not in the official ranking. Learn how the games are played and how the betting is organized in a casino.

Watch lots of tournaments before you start competing. You'll have more confidence if you are familiar with what is going on. Watch the strategy that each player is using and assess its effectiveness. Make notes. It will help you later to remember good strategies.

Make sure you fully understand the rules and the strategy for the tournament game before you play. Get a copy of the tournament rules and study them carefully.

Ensure that you understand all the jargon associated with poker tournaments. Lots of unfamiliar terms and slang words are used in poker (see Glossary). If you don't understand a word being used, ask the casino staff for an explanation.

Practise the game as much as possible. This doesn't have to cost you any money. You can do this at home. You can also organize private games with your friends along the lines of tournament games.

Compete in minor tournaments and gradually work your way up before taking on the professionals. Don't start with major tournaments, as the competition will be the best of the world.

Make sure you have plenty of sleep and are well relaxed before a tournament. During the tournament you will have to concentrate for around 10–12 hours, which is very tiring. The breaks are extremely short, typically ten minutes per one-and-a-half to two hours. During the break, get some fresh air and stretch your legs.

Avoid drinking alcohol as it slows down your reactions.

Keep a diary of your hands and how you and your competitors played. Analyse your games and how you played. This way you can learn from your mistakes. A diary can be particularly helpful if you play regularly in tournaments. You will often meet the same opponents in future competitions. By keeping a log of their strengths and weaknesses, you can improve your chances of beating them.

Aim to win the top prize. Don't sit back and relax when you know you've reached the prize level. A minor prize will be little more than your original stake.

Take advantage of the fact that you are playing against strangers. In your local card room you may not be the best player and your reputation may not intimidate other players. Your best friend may recognize the signs that you are bluffing. However, your competitors in the tournament will know nothing about your method of play or past blunders.

Don't be intimidated by your competitors. They may try to unnerve you by staring hard into your face. Learn to deal with such tactics. You may be up against strong competition with seasoned players who have won major tournaments but each game is different. Play to the best of your ability. It may just be enough to win.

Learn to assess the other players quickly. Look for their strengths and weaknesses. Even when you're not contending for the pot, closely watch how the other competitors are playing. Be prepared to revise your initial assessments.

Once you identify weak opponents, play aggressively against them.

If your game finishes earlier than others, watch the competition. You may gain valuable information about your competitors in the next round.

Don't waste chips. To stay in a game it is important to save your chips for your best plays. Staying in for one extra round of betting unnecessarily will cost you a lot of chips. If you have a poor hand and don't intend to bluff, fold it early.

Take advantage of buy-ins. Having more chips allows you to attack more and play aggressively. Being constantly worried about your chip level will make you more cautious.

If buy-ins of chips are allowed during the game, some players deliberately try to lose chips to participate in the buy-in. If you play aggressively at this time, you can easily accumulate their chips. Your own chip level will also determine whether it is worth losing chips to participate in a buy-in.

Adapt your play to suit each stage of the game. Play aggressively in the early stages to accumulate chips and intimidate the other players. Some players will be nervous. By appearing confident and intimidating them with aggressive play, you can push them out of a game.

It is possible to bluff more than usual. This is because players tend to be more cautious and fold more easily in tournaments. Your assessment of the players will give you a good indication of when to bluff.

Once you are in a comfortable position with a lot of chips, play more tightly. Save your attacks for your best hands. Let the other players battle among one another.

Attack players who are low on chips. They are more likely to fold to stay in the game.

Don't attack aggressive players. Battling with an aggressive player can cost you a lot of chips. Wait until they have folded, then concentrate on attacking the other players.

Learn to adapt your play to suit the game. If there are several aggressive players at the beginning of the game let them knock each other out. Once most of the competition has been eliminated you can start to attack.

Don't get over confident. You may be lucky with the draw and have poor competition on the first round but, as you progress to each new level in the tournament, the competition will be tougher.

If playing away from home, check the local tax laws. For example, in the United States non-resident aliens are taxed 30 per cent on gross winnings. Residents of some countries including the EEC and South Africa can claim exemption by completing IRS form 1001.

10

poker dice

Dice can also be used to play poker. Five dice are used. The faces of the dice are marked with ace, king, queen, jack, 10 and 9. Although the game can be played with two players, it is more practical when played with between three and six players.

figure 10.1 the symbols on the faces of the dice

The throws are ranked in the following descending order:

- five of a kind
- four of a kind
- full house
- high straight/big street
- low straight/small street
- three of a kind
- two pair
- one pair

The game is played with a cup/hat which covers the dice, and which sits on a felt-covered saucer. The equipment allows each player in turn to look at the dice without revealing them to the other players.

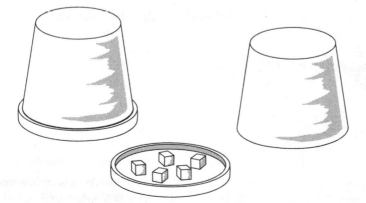

figure 10.2 the equipment for playing dice poker

Betting

There are several options for betting. Often the game is played in pubs for rounds of drinks. The loser is the one who buys a round for all the other players. Alternatively, the loser pays an agreed amount to each player.

Playing the game

Each player throws a dice, the one with the highest score goes first. The player puts all of the dice under the hat and shakes them. He announces his hand and passes the dice to the player sitting on either his left or right.

The game then continues in the direction selected (clockwise or anti-clockwise). The next player has the option of either accepting the throw or refusing it. If he refuses it, he removes the hat revealing the dice to all the other players. If the throw is equal to or more than that announced, the second player loses.

If the player accepts the throw, he must pass on a higher ranking throw to the next player. To get a higher ranking hand he is allowed to shake either all or some of the dice.

Dice may be removed from the hat and the remaining dice shaken, or dice may be left under the hat and some removed and thrown on the table. Players must always pass on a higher ranking hand. Even if you do not have a higher ranking hand, you can bluff.

Example game

Figure 10.3 shows the throws made by three players – A, B and C.

Player A goes first, he shakes all the dice, looks at what he has thrown and announces two jacks.

Player B accepts the throw and looks at the dice. He removes the jacks from the hat and places them on the table. He then shakes the remaining dice and looks at them. He announces two jacks, two tens and a nine.

Player C removes the two tens from the hat and places them on the table. The remaining dice is shaken in an attempt to get a full house. Although he fails to get a full house he has managed to beat B's throw. He announces two jacks, two tens and an ace.

Player A accepts this and also attempts to get a full house by shaking the remaining dice. He throws a jack and gets a full

figure 10.3 example of poker dice game

house. He announces three jacks and two tens or a full house jacks over tens.

Player B accepts. He removes the third jack from the hat and places it on the table. He puts the two tens under the hat and shakes the dice. To beat the full house he needs to throw two queens, two kings, two aces or another jack. He actually throws a king and a nine. This is not enough to beat the previous score so he lies and announces three jacks and two queens.

Player C refuses to accept and removes the hat. The bluff is revealed and player B loses.

Keeping score

Cards are usually used to keep the score. As the game is often played in pubs, beer mats are used. A player who loses a game receives a card. When all the cards have been used, players then return them when they win. The object of the game is to end up with no cards. The first player to get rid of all his cards is the winner. Players with no cards drop out of the game. The last player remaining is the loser.

Number of cards used

Players will usually agree between themselves how many cards will be used. As a rough guide, for two to three players six cards should be used and for four to six players, eight cards should be used.

With each new game the direction of play can be changed, as the first player decides whether to go clockwise or anti-clockwise. Once all the cards have been distributed, the direction of play can no longer be changed.

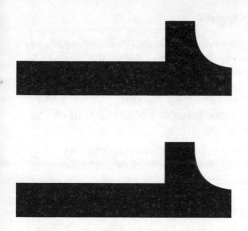

video poker machines

In this chapter you will learn:
- how to play video poker
- payout odds
- playing tips

What is video poker?

Video poker is a game based on five card draw. It is played on a machine, which displays the cards dealt much like a computer game. The player bets against the machine, which acts as the dealer and the banker. The object of the game is to make the highest-ranking poker hand possible. Video poker differs from most other slot machines because the skill of the player affects the outcome of the game.

A winning hand is paid a fixed return. The payouts for winning hands are displayed on the machine. The higher the ranking of the hand, the greater the returns. The payouts vary depending on where the game is played, in accordance with local legislation on gaming returns.

Video poker differs from a traditional game of five card draw in a number of ways:

- There is one player only so it is not necessary to beat other players' hands.
- It is a much faster game.
- The payout odds for particular hands are fixed.
- It does not involve bluffing.

Types of machine

There are a number of different types of machine with slight variations in the rules. The most popular games are jacks or better, deuces wild and joker wild. Games are also available where three hands at a time are played. For beginners jacks or better is a simpler game to play. The returns for a royal flush on some machines are fixed, on others there is a progressive jackpot, which accumulates each time a game is played. Machines with a fixed payout are called flat tops.

How to play

The aim is to make the highest-ranking poker hand possible that is in the payout schedule displayed on the machine. The minimum hand needed to win varies with different games.

The player inserts sufficient coins or a smart card to play. Smart cards are like credit cards that can be purchased and charged up with money at the cash-point. Minimum stakes are often in multiples of five coins. If you decide to play with fewer than five coins you will need to press the deal button. If you insert all five coins, the machine will automatically deal a five-card hand.

A standard deck of 52 cards is randomly shuffled and dealt as in a normal game of poker. The player receives a five-card hand. The player then has the opportunity to improve the hand by discarding cards and being dealt new ones.

The player decides which cards to keep and presses the corresponding hold button. A hold can be cancelled by pressing the button a second time. The player may keep all of the cards or discard any number of cards. It is possible to be dealt a winning hand with the initial five cards. This is usually indicated by a beep or a flashing light. When the player has decided which cards to keep, the draw/deal button is pressed. The machine will deal new cards to the hand. If a hand wins it will be paid out according to the payout schedule displayed on the machine.

Ranking of hands

Hands are ranked in the same way as five card draw (see page 20). For games where there are wild cards, additional hands that include the wild card, such as five of a kind, are allowed. A royal flush made with a wild card is considered a lower ranking hand than a regular royal flush.

Payout odds for different games

The odds given below are intended only as a guide and will vary depending on where the game is played.

Jacks or better

Jacks or better is the most popular game. To win you need to get a pair of jacks or better. The minimum stake is five coins.

Payout schedule

Hand	Payout per coin
Royal flush	250–800 or progressive jackpot
Straight flush	50
Four of a kind	25
Full house	6–9
Flush	5–6
Straight	4
Three of a kind	3
Two pair	2
Pair of jacks or better	1

Deuces wild

With deuces wild games, all twos are wild cards. This means that when you get a two you can use it to represent any card. If, for example, you have three aces and a two, the hand held will be counted as four aces. Because there is a greater chance of getting a ranking hand, only hands of three of a kind or better win.

Payout schedule

Hand	Payout per coin
Royal flush	Varies
Four deuces	200
Royal flush with deuces	25
Five of a kind	15
Straight flush	9
Four of a kind	5
Full house	3
Flush	2
Straight	2
Three of a kind	1

Joker wild

In the game of joker wild, an additional card of a joker is added to the deck, making 53 cards. The joker is a wild card. The additional joker makes it easier to achieve higher-ranking hands, which is reflected in lower payout odds than jacks or better. You also need to get a higher hand to win. You need at least two pair or better to win.

Payout schedule

Hand	Payout per coin
Royal flush	Varies
Five of a kind	100
Royal flush with joker	50
Straight flush	50
Four of a kind	20
Full house	8
Flush	7
Straight	5
Three of a kind	2
Two pair	1

Playing tips

Compare the payout schedules on each machine and select the best. Progressive machines offer the best value because they give you the opportunity to win a larger jackpot than flat top machines.

The overall return that a machine gives is usually expressed as a percentage. On some machines it is possible to get a return of over 100 per cent if they are played over a long term. Look for a machine that has already accumulated a large jackpot. In order to win the jackpot around 45 hours of fast play is required. This requires a bankroll of several thousand coins. If a large jackpot has already accumulated it will be possible to win it in a shorter time.

Always play the maximum possible stake as a smaller bet pays out lower odds. The maximum possible bet is usually five coins. A jackpot with five coins inserted pays on average 4000 coins. With only one coin inserted it pays around 250.

Learn the playing strategy for video poker. This differs from traditional five card draw because with video poker there is no bluffing involved. Strategies such as keeping a kicker to a pair are inappropriate for video poker.

Master jacks or better before graduating to other games. This is the simplest game to learn.

Make sure the strategy you use is the correct one for the game you are playing. Games with wild cards like deuces and joker wild are more complex and require a different strategy from jacks or better.

Play slowly and carefully while you are learning. Hands like straights are not always immediately obvious, as the cards will rarely be displayed in the correct ascending or descending order. Don't forget that in a straight an ace can be used as a high or a low card.

Basic strategy for jacks or better

The list below gives a simple strategy for jacks or better which is suitable for beginners.

1   Hold any hand of a straight or over in the ranking.
2   If four cards to a royal flush are held – draw one (including to a winning flush).

3 Four cards to a straight flush or a flush – draw one.
4 Three of a kind – draw two.
5 Two pair – draw one.
6 Pair – draw three.
7 Three card royal flush – draw two.
8 Four card straight – draw one.
9 Three card straight flush – draw two.
10 Two high cards J, Q, K, A – draw three.
11 Three high cards (Jack and over) – hold two of the same suit. If different suits, hold the two lowest high cards.
12 Four card straight – draw one.
13 High card – draw four.
14 Nothing – draw five.

12

internet poker

In this chapter you will learn:
- the equipment required
- costs
- how to play

What is internet poker?

Internet poker is playing the game on a computer via an internet connection. This means you can play in the comfort of your own home against players from all over the world. Both video poker and traditional games of poker can be played. There are lots of gambling sites on the internet that offer these facilities. In addition, there are sites where it is possible to play for fun.

Video poker and Caribbean stud poker can be played in a similar way to the casino version. The player deposits money into an on-line account and can then gamble. Any winnings are paid into the account, which can then be transferred to a bank account.

A choice of traditional poker games can be played including hold 'em, seven card stud and omaha. The websites that offer traditional games of poker link up players from around the world. Each player logs into the game. The cards are electronically dealt. Players have a time limit to make a decision about their hand. Bets are made from and winnings paid into an on-line account.

With internet poker you cannot see your competitors so it is more difficult to assess whether or not someone is bluffing. You also have the advantage that the other competitors cannot see you. This may change as the technology for video conferencing develops.

Is it legal?

The legality of internet gambling depends on where you live. The internet is a new medium for gambling and legislation has been slow to keep pace with new developments. In the United Kingdom internet gambling is legal and there are proposals to license operators. United States federal law, notably the Wire Act, prohibits internet gambling. However, some states such as Nevada have legalized it. In Australia the government has a system in place to license on-line gambling.

Where gambling is illegal, prosecutions tend to be mostly against the operators of gaming sites. If you intend to bet on the internet you need to take particular care with whom you bet. If you are gambling with a site that is subsequently closed down you could lose your money.

How fair is it?

There have been concerns raised as to the fairness of on-line poker games because many sites are unregulated. The number of unfair sites far outweighs the fair ones. If you decide to bet over the internet, take care to shop around for a good site. If possible select a government licensed website. Alternatively look for a company with a good reputation.

There are lots of websites that contain details of blacklisted on-line casinos. Before you gamble check that your intended website is not on the list. Also check how long the website has been operating. A website that has been operating for a number of years without getting blacklisted is a safer bet.

Organizations such as the Interactive Gaming Council and Safebet vet on-line gambling sites. They have a code of conduct for members, customer complaint services and a mediation department to resolve disputes. They publish lists of on-line gaming sites that meet their strict criteria. Safebet also carries out random checks of the software used by gambling sites to ensure that it is fair.

Look for a site that actively combats cheating and permanently bars those caught. Collusion is the most obvious way for players to cheat. Theoretically an individual player with several computers can cheat in this manner. A good site will use computer programs to analyse the games and permanently bar players who are caught colluding. Another potential problem is for abuse of the all-in rule. Look for a site that limits the number of times that this rule can be used.

Treat betting on the internet with caution and bet only if you are certain that you have found a fair website.

Equipment required

You will need a computer and internet connection. Make sure you fully understand how to operate your computer before starting. Pressing the wrong button and disconnecting yourself midway through a game can lose you money. You will need to be able to download software and install it on your computer. Once the software is installed you will need to know how to find it and operate it on your computer.

Also familiarize yourself with the internet. Many sites have similar names. If you register with a site, keep a note of its full

URL so that you can find it again. Also note the password that you use and keep it secret. If other people have access to your computer don't request your computer to remember your password. If you do the other users will be able to log in and play with your money.

Costs

In addition to the cost of the bets you will have to pay for the hardware (computer equipment) and the internet connection. The website will make a charge based either on the number of bets made or on a percentage of the amount bet. The rake varies with different sites; around five per cent or less is typical. The software (computer program) for playing the games is usually given to you free by the gambling site.

If you use a credit card, debit card or on-line bank account to bet, you will incur charges for transferring the money. If you mail money you will have postage costs. Depending on where you live you may have to pay local betting taxes.

How to play

You will need to register with an on-line gambling site. This usually involves completing a registration form giving personal details such as name, address, telephone number, email address and bank or credit card details. The games are played using pseudonyms or nicknames, so you will be asked to select a name. An account will be set up for you so that you can track bets made and winnings deposited. To start betting you will need to deposit sufficient funds into the website account. This can either be mailed to the website or deposited with a credit card, debit card or bank transfer.

You will need to download the software and install it on to your computer. Most programs include a version of the game that can be played at home for free that will allow you to practise and familiarize yourself with the rules. A variety of games can be played. Make sure you fully understand the rules and how to operate the game before you begin to play.

When you join a game you will need to stay on-line until the completion of the game. If your connection is lost there are rules to protect the bets made so far. The all-in rule means that you will still have a chance to win the pot to which you have contributed. A new pot is then started for the players remaining in the game. At the end of the game, your hand will be compared against the winning hand and you will win that portion of the pot to which you contributed.

On-line tournaments

On-line tournaments offer the chance to play for a small stake and potentially to win a large prize. There are lots of on-line tournaments. Some are free to enter. It is even possible to play on-line for a place in a major tournament such as the World Series of Poker.

glossary

ante a bet made before any cards have been dealt

babies small value cards

bicycle *see* wheel

big blind the minimum bet on the first round of betting

blind bet a bet made without looking at your cards

bluff tricking the other players into thinking that you have a really good hand

board the community cards in games such as hold 'em and omaha

bone another name for a chip

bug a joker

bullet an ace

burnt card a card which is removed from the pack and not used in play. Often several of the top cards will be removed before hands are dealt to combat cheating by the dealer

button a plastic marker used in casino games to denote an imaginery dealer to ensure that no player gains an advantage from his position relative to the actual dealer

by me a verbal statement in draw poker that a player is not exchanging any cards

call a verbal statement that a player will match the previous bet

calling station a player who hardly ever raises

chip a plastic disc used in place of money for betting

commission a charge made by the casino for the use of its facilities, usually a percentage of the pot

community cards cards which can be used by all the players to make up their best five card poker hand in games such as hold 'em and omaha

dead man's hand two pair of aces over eights

deuce two

door card in stud poker the first card that is dealt face up

draw exchanging cards in your hand for cards from the deck

fives five cards of the same value – this hand is only possible where wild cards are used

flat tops video poker machines with fixed payout odds

flop the deal where the first three community cards are revealed in hold 'em and omaha

flush five cards of the same suit

fold withdraw from the game

fours four cards of the same value, for example, four queens

freak a wild card

full house three cards of the same value with a pair, for example, three aces and two sixes

hole cards a player's cards which are dealt face down

house advantage an adjustment made to the odds on banking games which allows the casino to make a profit

kicker in draw poker this is a card retained to make it more difficult for your opponents to guess your hand

knave a jack

knock in draw poker a player may knock on the table to signify that no cards are required

limit the maximum bet

low poker a game where players aim to have the lowest ranking poker hand

marked cards cards which have been marked in some way so that a cheat can identify their values from looking at their backs

monster a high ranking hand

muck pile the pile of cards from players who have folded

nuts having a hand in games such as hold 'em and omaha which is the best possible hand and which cannot be beaten by any other player

odds a ratio expressing your chances of losing against your chances of winning, for example, odds of 2/1 means you have two chances of losing against 1 chance of winning

open to place the first bet

openers cards needed to open a pot, for example, two jacks are needed to open a jackpot. In some games, a minimum hand is needed before an opening bet can be made. In a jackpot, two jacks are needed, for a queen pot – two queens, etc.

over used as a short way of expressing two pair, for example, queens over tens means two queens and two tens

paint any court card, for example, king, queen or jack

pig a high and low hand

pocket cards cards which are dealt face down

poker face having complete control over your facial expressions so that you do not give your opponents any clues about your hand

pokies video poker machines

progressives video poker machines with increasing jackpots

rake a charge made by the casino for the use of its facilities, usually a percentage of the pot

river the last round of betting

rock a player who always folds unless he has a really good hand

run another name for a straight

runt a hand lower than a pair

school a group of players who regularly play poker together

see has the same meaning as 'call'

set three cards of the same value

showdown when the players reveal their hands

sitting pat a player who takes no cards in draw poker

stake the amount of money bet

straddle a method of betting where the previous bet is doubled – the doubling of previous bets usually continues for a pre-determined number of times

straight five cards of any suit in consecutive order

street a round of betting – first street is the first round of betting, second street the second and so on

stud a form of poker where some cards are dealt face up

sweeten to add money to the pot, usually in the form of an ante-bet

technician someone who is skilled at manipulating the cards so that he can deal himself a good hand

threes three cards of the same value

trey a three

trips three cards of the same value

wheel 5, 4, 3, 2, A in low poker

wild cards a nominated card which can be used in place of any other card to form a poker hand

Useful contact details

SafeBet Organisation Inc.
9030 W. Sahara Avenue
Las Vegas
Nevada
Zip 89117-5744
USA
Tel: 877-471-4153
Email support@safebet.org
www.safebet.org
A non-profit gaming organization that monitors member casinos to ensure they abide by the rules and regulations set by safe bet.

How to Win
The website of Belinda Levez
www.click.to/howtowin

Gamblers Anonymous organizations in Great Britain, Australia and the United States

Great Britain
Gamblers Anonymous
National Service Office
PO Box 88
London
SW10 0EU
Tel: 08700 50 88 80
www.gamblersanonymous.org.uk

United States
Gamblers Anonymous
PO Box 13173
Los Angeles
CA90017
Tel: 213 386-8789
www.gamblersanonymous.org/index.html

Australia
Gamblers Anonymous
Head Office
Corner of Dorcas and Montague Street
South Melbourne
Tel: 03 9696 6108

Gamblers Anonymous
PO Box Burwood
Sydney
NSW 2134
Tel: 02 9564 1574
www.gamblersanonymous.org.au